Wicked Strange

WICKED STRANGE

Your Guide to Ghosts, Monsters, Oddities & Urban Legends from New England

Jeff Belanger

Photography by Frank C. Grace

This edition first published in 2025
by New Page Books, an imprint of
Red Wheel/Weiser, LLC
With offices at:
65 Parker Street, Suite 7
Newburyport, MA 01950

www.redwheelweiser.com

ISBN: 978-1-63748-021-2

Interior design and digital illustration by Sky Peck Design
Typeset in Weiss

Printed in China

WM

10 9 8 7 6 5 4 3 2 1

LIBRARY OF CONGRESS CATALOGING-IN-PUBLICATION DATA

Names: Belanger, Jeff, author. Title: Wicked strange : your guide to ghosts, monsters, oddities, and urban legends from New England / Jeff Belanger ; with photographs by Frank C. Grace.
Description: Newburyport, MA : New Page, [2025] | Includes index.
| Summary: "A celebration of all the things that make New England like no other place on earth, this travel guide will take readers on an expedition to the strange and frequently unseen world that is often right under their noses. It explores numerous haunted places, environs where mysterious creatures were spotted, locations where unusual events happened, and roadside the oddities along the way. Journey through the towns, hamlets, and hills that hide the strangest of history and uncover the wickedly strange"-- Provided by publisher. Identifiers: LCCN 2024047510 | ISBN 9781637480212 (trade paperback) | ISBN 9781633413795 (ebook)
Subjects: LCSH: Haunted places--New England. | Ghosts--New England. | Curiosities and wonders--New England. | Legends-- New England. | New England--Guidebooks.
Classification: LCC BF1472.U6 B455 2025 | DDC 133.10974--dc23/eng/20250106
LC record available at https://lccn.loc.gov/2024047510

CREDITS:

Panorama of the Molasses Disaster site. Globe Newspaper Co. (1919). Boston Public Library. Public domain, via Wikimedia Commons.
Thomas Cole (1801-1848), A View of the Mountain Pass Called the Notch of the White Mountains (Crawford Notch). Public domain, via Wikimedia Commons.
"Vision of the Phantom Ship, 1647" by Jesse Talbot (circa 1850). Public domain. New Haven Historical Society via Wikimedia Commons.
English Jack – The Hermit of the White Mountains. Used by permission of the New Hampshire Historical Society.
The Ghost of Nancy Barton, Crawford Notch, New Hampshire. Used by permission of the Appalachian Mountain Club.
The hermit of Monhegan Island, ME. Spencer Grant / Alamy Stock Photo
"Make Mine Moxie." 1950's Moxie advertisement featuring baseball player Ted Williams. Edward Roth / Alamy Stock Photo

For Sophie. I've loved watching you grow up
in this strange land called New England.
Your inquisitive mind and open heart inspire me every day.
I'm honored to be your dad.

—J. B.

For Nathan and Nicholas.
I love you guys more than anything.
I am so proud to be your wicked strange dad.

—F. C. G.

Contents

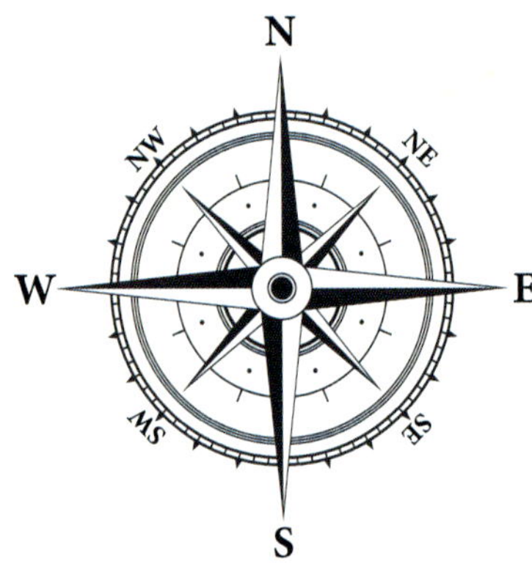

Acknowledgments • x

Introduction • 1

CONNECTICUT

Born: January 9, 1788

May God Strike Me Down: The Curious Grave of David Sherman—Bridgeport • 4

Mark Twain's Haunted Mansion—Hartford • 7

The Battle of the Frogs—Willimantic • 9

The Sleeping Giant—Hamden • 10

The Lordship Sea Serpent and Mermaid—Stratford • 12

The Nation's Most Controversial First Hamburger—New Haven • 15

The UFO Crash at Bantam Lake—Morris • 17

Yo Ho Ho and a Burial of Rum—Lebanon • 18

Bank Street's Haunted Stove—New Milford • 19

They Only Moved the Headstones—New London • 21

The Shoebox Murder Mystery—Wallingford • 23

The Glawackus—Glastonbury • 25

The Black Dog of Meriden—Meriden • 27

The Ghost Ship of New Haven Harbor—New Haven • 31

Gungywamp—Groton • 32

The Darn Man—Hampton • 35

The Haunted Piano of Gardner Lake—Salem • 36

MASSACHUSETTS

Born: February 6, 1788

The Westford Knight—Westford • 40

Forklore on Old Harbor Road—Westport • 42

Lizzie Borden Took an Axe—Fall River • 44

Persecuted for Wearing a Beard—Leominster • 46

The Great Molasses Flood—Boston • 47

Witch Bonney Awaits—Lowell • 50

The Sea Serpent of Gloucester and Rockport—Gloucester and Rockport • 51

Boston's Big Steaming Tea Kettle—Boston • 53

Dogtown's Inspirational Boulders—Gloucester • 54

Have a Nice Day . . . and Afterlife—Worcester • 57

A Mill Run by Satanic Imps—Easton • 59

A Skeleton in Armor—Fall River • 62

Ripton: Massachusetts's Most Mysterious Town—Berkshire County • 64

One If by Land, Two If by Sea . . . Three If by Air?—Boston • 67

Timothy Dexter: An Idiot Who Failed Upward—Newburyport • 68

New England's First Documented UFO—Boston • 71

Edith Wharton's Haunted Mount—Lenox • 73

NEW HAMPSHIRE

Born: June 21, 1788

A Tombstone Tirade—Milford • 76

A Redstone Missile on the Town Green—Warren • 78

The Haunted Mt. Washington Hotel—Bretton Woods • 80

English Jack—The Hermit of the White Mountains—Crawford Notch • 82

Chicken Farmer, I Still Love You—Newbury • 84

The Great Wall of Sandwich—Sandwich • 87

A Sermon from Beer Bottle Church—Hampton Falls • 90

Ruth Colbath: A Woman Who Waited—Albany • 93

It Gives Us the "Willeys"—Crawford Notch • 95

The Immortal Doc Benton—Mt. Moosilauke • 98

A Contract for Murder with the Devil—Somersworth • 100

A Haunted Lake . . . Literally—Francestown • 103

The Devil's Baked Beans—Lyndeborough • 107

The Ghost of Nancy Barton—Crawford Notch • 110

Madame Sherri's Castle Ruins—Chesterfield • 114

America's Stonehenge—Salem • 117

Betty and Barney Hill's UFO Incident—Lincoln • 120

RHODE ISLAND

Born: May 29, 1790

The Legendary Fountain of Benefit Street—Providence • 124
The Cumberland Vampire—Cumberland • 126
Stephen Smith's Heartbreak House—Lincoln • 128
Should Have Been the Wife of Simeon Palmer—Little Compton • 131
She Laughed Herself to Death—Newport • 134
An Explosion Jarred Some Passengers—Providence • 134
Cranston's Headless Corpse—Cranston • 135
The Woonsocket Werewolf—Woonsocket • 138
The Haunting of Conimicut Lighthouse—Warwick • 140
The Burning Beast of Glocester—Glocester • 142
The Floating Heads of Kickemuit River—Warren • 144
The Bell Still Tolls at the Ram Tail Factory—Foster • 146
The Moaning Bones of Mt. Tom—Exeter • 148
The Narragansett Rune Stone—North Kingstown • 149
The Northern Rhode Island UFO Flap of 1967—Woonsocket • 150
Purgatory Chasm's Lover's Leap—Middletown • 153
Rhode Island's Brokenhearted Tower—South Kingstown • 154

VERMONT

Born: March 4, 1791

Emily's Haunted Bridge—Stowe • 158
The Curse of Black Agnes—Montpelier • 160
File This Under "Strange"—Burlington • 162
Vermont's Sweetest Cemetery—Waterbury • 164
The Wampahoofus—Mt. Mansfield • 167
A Bad Case of Taphephobia—New Haven • 168
I Want My Mummy—Middlebury • 170
Queen Connie and the Beetle—Leicester • 171
The Phineas Gage Incident—Cavendish • 172
Champ the Lake Monster—Lake Champlain • 173
The Curse of the Cemetery Vine—East Dummerston • 175
The Buff Ledge Camp UFO Abduction—Colchester • 178
Who's Buried in Ethan Allen's Tomb?—Burlington • 178
An Ice Age Monster from the Deep—Brandon • 181
Vermont's Haunted Police Academy—Pittsford • 183
A Haunted Tower in the Woods—Brattleboro • 184
Little Maggie: Newport's Fisherwoman—Newport • 185
The Bellows Falls Petroglyphs—Bellows Falls • 187

MAINE

Born: March 15, 1820

The Haunting of Portland Head Lighthouse—Cape Elizabeth • 190
The Big Birth of Paul Bunyan—Bangor • 192
A Witch's Curse on Colonel Buck's Grave—Bucksport • 193
Bill Knights's Ghost Haunts Rufie Brown—West Athens • 194
America's Last Crank Call—Woodstock • 195
The Hoodoo Hearse of Holden—Holden • 197
Maine's Sistine Chapel—South Solon • 200
Maine's Stolen Governor—Augusta • 202
The Allagash UFO Incident—Allagash Wilderness • 205
A Nerve Tonic that Launched a War—Union • 206
The Leaping Lumberjacks of Central Maine—Moosehead Lake • 209
The Specter Moose of Lobster Lake—Piscataquis • 210
Razor Shins—Aroostook County • 211
The Pamola—Mt. Katahdin • 213
The Phantom of the Opera House—Boothbay • 215
The Hermit of Manana Island—Monhegan Island • 216
The Billdad—Skinner • 218

Index • 220
About Jeff and Frank • 227

Acknowledgments

Jeff Belanger:

I first met photographer Frank Grace in 2012 at the haunted Lizzie Borden House in Fall River, Massachusetts. I was there for an event that evening and was excited to meet him! Like many of us weirdoes, I had seen Frank's photography online. He loves photographing the same types of places I love researching and writing about. Frank was there, with his camera in hand, shooting the house and the event. I approached him and said, "Hey, man, I love your photography!"

He pointed to the shutter on his camera. "I just push this button," he said. "The camera does most of the work." And so began a friendship and partnership that continues to this day. You might even say our relationship hit a crescendo with this very book you're holding right now. I tell creepy and weird stories with words; Frank does it with his photos. Frank has always been up for a road trip, adventure, ghost hunt, producing an annual haunted New England calendar, a haunted stage show, *Wicked Strange New England* book, or any other odd project that comes our way. Thank you, Frank! I've learned so much about photography from you. I'm in awe of the way you can tell a story with an image.

Thank you to Tony Dunne, my *New England Legends* television series partner for PBS and Amazon Prime. It all began with you back in 2012! Thanks to Ray Auger, my *New England Legends* podcast cohost and partner. Every week we get together to explore some (wicked) strange New England oddity. The podcast was a huge inspiration for this book. Thank you to John Judd and Lauren Middleton, who round out the *New England Legends* family.

A big thank-you to everyone who has been watching the *New England Legends* television series and listening to the weekly podcast. So many of our story leads come from you! This community of legend-seekers has grown into something truly special. I'm proud to be part of it and appreciate every weird tip, email, and social media post anyone has ever shared with me. Keep them coming!

Thank you to Scott Wheeler from Vermont's *Northland Journal* for your help with Little Maggie. Thank you to Sarah Galligan from the New Hampshire Historical Society, thanks to Michael Pye, Christine LeBlond, Diana Drew, Jane Hagaman, and Kathryn Sky-Peck at New Page Books for turning our vision into art.

Thank you to my wife, Megan, for supporting me throughout the grueling process of birthing this book. You've always been my first reader, my first editor, and my rock for everything I do. Every time I have a crazy idea, you're the first to suggest I chase it. I couldn't do any of this without you. Thank you for all of the love and support over the years. Thank you to my daughter, Sophie, for joining me on some of my weird adventures and for being proud of your dad's strange job. Finally, thanks to my family for always believing in me, and for having the good sense to ensure I was born a Masshole in New England.

Frank C. Grace:

When I first visited the haunted location of my hometown's most enduring legend, the unsolved Borden Family murders, little did I know it would reignite my passion for—and dark obsession with—all that is wicked strange in New England and beyond. I blame and thank Tim Weisberg of *Spooky Southcoast* for introducing me to Jeff Belanger. Jeff's memory of our first meeting is spot-on, one of those fond memories associated with a location. I was already familiar with his work, specifically the internet show *30 Odd Minutes*, and I was a little surprised when he said he knew of me! But, things changed when he said, "Hey, what do you think about working on a haunted New England calendar?" It snowballed from there into working together on small projects to a stage show production, all the while cementing a friendship and mutual respect, all on a haunted foundation. The countless road trips, discussions, and projects have all led to this book. So thanks, Jeff, for being who you are and for building the *New England Legends* community. I cannot think of a better-suited author to bring my images to life. Your words and my photos create a certain spooky synergy.

A huge thank-you as well to all the *New England Legends* community that keep us supplied with stories and leads. As Jeff said, so many of these stories came right from you! More thanks in our Legendary community go out to Tony Dunne, Ray Auger, Laura Middleton, and John Judd, who are incredibly valuable in shaping these stories and overall projects.

I'd also like to thank the following for the information you have been able to provide as well as location access for photography: Andy Davis and the South Solon Historical Society (South Solon, Maine), Michael Martins and the Fall River Historical Society, Jacques Lamarre (your company at the Mark Twain House will never be forgotten), Ellen Rainville and the J. V. Fletcher Library (Westford, Massachusetts), the late and missed Lee-Ann Wilbur, Kathy Hartley and the Hearthside House Museum (Lincoln, Rhode Island), George Gross at the Matthews Museum of Maine Heritage, Carl Johnson (our lead on the Floating Heads story), and the University of New Hampshire (which provided access to the Hill UFO archives).

Thanks to my dad, another Frank Grace, for leaving UFO books and paranormal books lying around the house when I was a kid. You're kinda at fault for this book as well!

But, most importantly, I'd like to thank my wife, Bonnie, for all the snacks, drinks, and sandwiches she made so I wouldn't perish during some seven-hundred-mile and twelve-hour days taking photos for this book. She also had to put up with listening to my legend-tripping journeys when I got back and viewing my edits. I love you more than you could ever know. The same goes for our sons, Nathan and Nicholas. They heard and had to endure all the overly dramatic descriptions of what I saw and shot. They were even able to get me closer to places I had to shoot, like Bridgewater State University track meets with Nicholas and Red Sox games in Boston with Nathan. I will always fondly remember who I was with or was going to see when I took certain photos for the book. I love you guys and am more proud of you than you know. And I cannot forget the loving creature that was in the room with me during all these photo edits. She'd lie on the floor and pick her head up when I got visibly excited and at times jumped in my lap for a quick lick of my face for encouragement. Special thanks to Zoe, our Mini-Australian Shepherd, for always being there.

Introduction

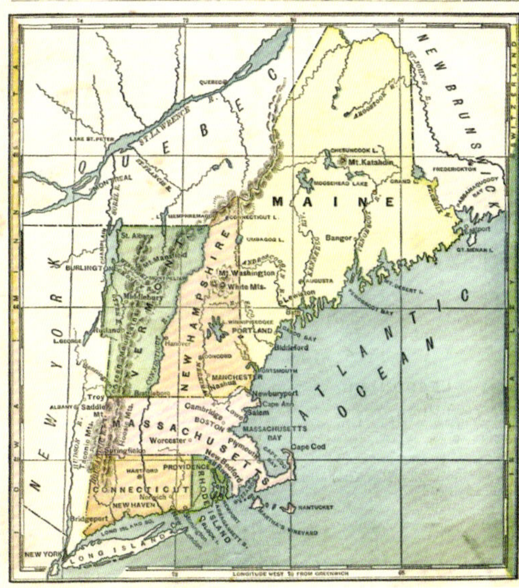

New England was a perfectly normal place until about twelve thousand years ago when the first people arrived . . . since then, things have gotten wicked strange. People, it turns out, tend to leave behind a mark. Sometimes a scar. Our ancestors have left us signs and messages from the past. Some of those messages are scary, some messages are cryptic and open to interpretation, and others are hysterical.

What follows are a series of those messages from the past. We call them legends.

Have you ever heard a story about a haunted place, a monster lurking somewhere dark and spooky, or talk of extraterrestrials visiting our world? Maybe you've read a story about an ancient site whose purpose has never been fully explained to everyone's satisfaction. Ever been driving along and seen a roadside oddity someone erected for no other reason than to scream, "I was here and I made this weird thing!"? Perhaps you've heard about some eccentric person who lived their lives so unconventionally that we're still talking about them today. Or maybe you've visited a burial ground where a specific tomb cried out for more attention than all of its neighbors. If so, you've come to the right place. New England is full of legends like these.

A legend is a living, breathing thing. It's the story that evolves around a peculiar event that we're still trying to make sense of. A legend can be born, it can marry another, it can relocate, and it can die. However, the only way a legend dies is when we stop talking about it. The legends in your hands right now are still very much alive.

If we trace the story back far enough, we find there's truth in it. Someone had a profound experience they couldn't explain at a specific location, so they tell their story. Others investigate the story's ground zero for themselves and then become part of that story. They write themselves into the book. Maybe they have an experience they also can't explain, or maybe they leave scratching their head.

Many of these legends you're about to read are a sermon from the past. We have yet to fully reconcile or explain what happened, even if it was long ago, so we continue to discuss it. In a way, that makes people like us, your humble author and photographer, ministers of the weird.

Maybe it's the winters. In New England, we tend to hibernate and share stories while we protect ourselves from the sometimes bitter cold outside. Maybe it's because we hold on to the past here. We clutch traditions and beliefs the way some people hang on to old coats. Sure, it may not look the way it once did, but those tears, mends, and stains add character to a perfectly comfortable garment, even if it's hard to recognize the original at this point.

Wicked Strange is a journey and a celebration of all the things that make New England like no other place on Earth. From the Indigenous people to early pilgrims seeking refuge to our neighbors who paint their faces for sporting events today, we have many centuries and layers of history and beliefs that can still be found swirling in the *chowdah* that is New England. In a time when so much of the world is becoming homogenized—as big-box stores and chain restaurants move in, and so many communities lose their identity—we still have these legends. They belong to specific towns and streets. These are stories locals will share with you . . . if they trust you.

You might ask: What's our source on these legends? The short answer is you.

Jeff and Frank will be your guides. We're one part objective reporter—documenting and always looking for the root of a legend, where it started, and how it grew—and one part active participant. If the story says you knock three times on the cursed headstone at midnight under a full moon, bet your campfire and roasted marshmallow we'll at least try it, because part of us will always wonder, *What if?*

In the coming pages, we'll take you on a cemetery safari through New England's old boneyards, where we'll explore odd epitaphs and memorable monuments. We'll gawk at the roadside oddities, investigate the haunts, and meet the people who have been the croutons in the salad that is America's Northeast. We're embarking on a journey to the strange and often-unseen world that frequently sits, unassuming, right beneath our noses. These are tales so strange you might not believe them if you didn't see them for yourself.

So go ahead and flip to any page. Begin anywhere you like. Oddities are everywhere. The wicked strange begs us to step closer, take a long gander, and ask big questions.

Connecticut

Born: January 9, 1788

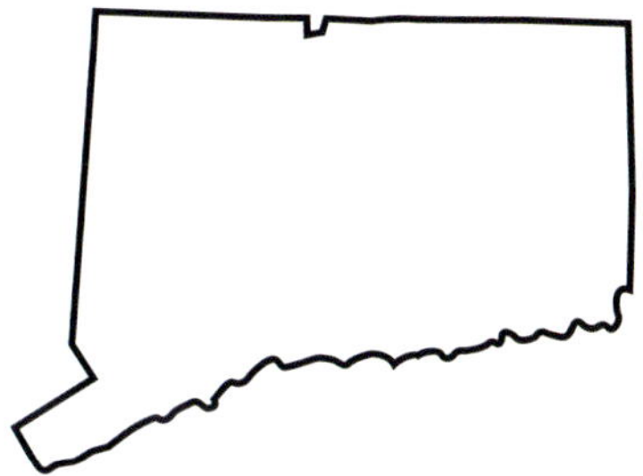

We're exploring Connecticut's weirdness first because the "Nutmeg State" was the first to earn statehood in New England. Connecticut is the land of other firsts, too. The license plate reads CONSTITUTION STATE because 19th-century Connecticut historian John Fiske claimed the Fundamental Orders of 1638 and 1639 were the first written constitution in history. Folks have argued that fact since, but no matter. It's on the license plate now, and there's no arguing with a license plate.

It's been called the Nutmeg State because when that spice first landed in Connecticut's ports from the East Indies, locals went nuts for the flavor in their pies and cooking. You make the spice by grating the hardened seed into powder. When others around the country wanted to get their hands on them, some Connecticut merchants took to selling carved wooden "seeds" and passing them off as counterfeit nutmeg—a shady way to earn a nickname, we know.

In 1908, New Haven candymaker George Smith pushed sticks into hard candies as they cooled and solidified. He named this treat after a local racehorse he'd seen named "Lolly Pop," and an icon was born.

Whether looking at that strange border-dispute notch (also called the Southwick Jog or Granby Notch, depending on which side you live on) along Connecticut's northern border, which it shares with Massachusetts, or exploring its boneyards, haunts, restaurants, and roadside oddities, Connecticut is full of high strangeness.

May God Strike Me Down

The Curious Grave of David Sherman

BRIDGEPORT, CONNECTICUT

It's a long-standing joke in our family: We don't go to church anymore because we're afraid lightning will strike and someone innocent could be killed. But it's just a joke, right? *Ha ha?*

If you take a stroll through Old Stratfield Cemetery in Bridgeport, Connecticut, you'll see historic graves, some dating back to the 1690s, back to when this boneyard was known as Pequonnock Cemetery. There are Revolutionary War heroes buried in this small park, town-founding fathers and mothers, but also the curious grave of a man who was struck down by lightning . . . *while attending church*!

We know from a glance at the headstone, adorned at the top with a traditional New England death head, that David Sherman was born circa 1736. But the epitaph is the most showstopping among a field of old headstones:

HERE LYES BURIED THE BODY OF MR. DAVID SHERMAN WHO WAS KILLED BY LIGHTNING IN THE HOUSE OF GOD AT PUBLICK WORSHIP ON THE 28TH OF JULY 1771 IN THE 35TH YEAR OF HIS AGE.

What?!

When we saw this headstone, we doubled down on our stay-out-of-church convictions. However, we had to know more, so we went digging through history. We were shocked to learn that David was *not* the only victim that fateful day at Sunday service.

First, we found the journal of William Wheeler who penned: *A Journal for the Town of Fairfield, or An exact & impartial Account of the most Material Transactions from the first Settlement thereof till the Present Time.*

He saw fit to mention David Sherman's demise as a notable event in town; in fact, the only notable event for the year 1771:

"July—The Lightning struck Stratfield meetinghouse & killed uncle John Burr & ripped open the Shoes of his brother Ozias that stood near him & killed likewise David Sherman."

From there we found the book: *A General History of The Burr Family in America with a Genealogical Record from 1570 to 1878* by Charles Burr Todd. This book offered more details:

"Captain John Burr, a farmer, son of Col. John Burr, was killed by lightning at the old Pequonnock meeting house, July 28, 1771. The congregation was standing in prayer. Parson Rose stopped praying, and after a pause he uttered the following words, 'Are we all here?' When the congregation moved out it was found that David Sherman and John Burr were dead. They were both in the prime of life, with families (the very pick of the flock). There was no rod on the steeple at that time."

No lightning rod, and these two poor gents are struck down during services, and poor Ozias lost a shoe! "Are we all here?" No, we are *not*! Still, we're curious how Parson Rose's collection plate did that unforgettable Sunday in 1771.

Here lyes Buried
the Body of
Mr DAVID SHERMAN
Who was Kill'd by Lightning in the
Houſe of God at publick worſhip
on the 28th of July 1771 in ye
35th Year of His Age

Mark Twain's Haunted Mansion

HARTFORD, CONNECTICUT

Then away out in the woods I heard that kind of a sound that a ghost makes when it wants to tell about something that's on its mind and can't make itself understood, and so can't rest easy in its grave, and has to go about that way every night grieving.

—MARK TWAIN

Huckleberry Finn knew about ghosts, as did his creator, American literary treasure Samuel Clemens, better known by his pen name, Mark Twain.

Between 1874 and 1891, Mark Twain lived in this stately Hartford home with his wife and three daughters. During his stay in Hartford, Twain penned some of his greatest works, including *Adventures of Huckleberry Finn*, *The Adventures of Tom Sawyer*, and *A Connecticut Yankee in King Arthur's Court*. Mark Twain called his years in this home the happiest and most productive years of his life.

Life *was* good for Twain. Until 1891, when financial problems forced him to move to Europe where he could earn more money on speaking tours. While overseas, tragedy struck the family. In 1896, Twain's beloved daughter Susy, who stayed behind in their Hartford home, died from meningitis at age twenty-four. The family thought it would be too difficult to live in Hartford again without Susy, so the mansion was sold in 1903. The building later served as a boarding school, library, and then a museum dedicated to Mark Twain.

The most prominent ghostly figure in the home today is that of a young woman in a long white dress who has been seen gliding along the hallways, stairways, and hovering in Susy's former bedroom. We can only speculate that this is the spirit of Twain's daughter, returning to the place she was happiest. Employees of the museum acknowledge that there's a spirit to the building, and they often feel like they're not alone inside . . . if only the mansion's ghost could make itself understood.

In his book, *A Connecticut Yankee in King Arthur's Court*, Twain wrote: "None but the dead are permitted to tell the truth."

The Battle of the Frogs

WILLIMANTIC, CONNECTICUT

The South Street Bridge that spans the Willimantic River in downtown Willimantic is adorned with two giant frog statues at either end, sitting atop spool pillars. The most newsworthy part of this story is that the state of Connecticut agreed to pay for not just the bridge, but also the art. Maybe they were sold on the historical significance of the Battle of the Frogs—the deadliest war you've never heard of.

Though you weren't told about this infamous battle in school, know that countless lives were lost, a town shook in fear, and a commemorative plaque was placed lest we ever forget what happened back in July of 1758.

The summer of 1758 had been hot and dry. The region around Willimantic was in a horrible drought. To compound the stress, the French and Indian War had been raging for four years. Connecticut troops were active in battles in nearby New York State, and folks were wondering when the war would come to their own backyards. They received the answer sooner than anyone was ready for.

One afternoon in July, dark storm clouds covered the skies. Soon, the clouds opened up, with torrential rain pouring down onto the dry earth below. After hours of downpour, the storm moved off, leaving the world cooled and soaked. It was much needed and appreciated. But then, as night fell, the folks in nearby Old Windham heard something horrific in the distance.

At Parson White's house, his servant in his quarters outside suddenly heard women and children shrieking as if being tortured, so he alerted the parson. Soon, others in town also heard the massacre. They could also hear French soldiers screaming out the names of specific men in Old Windham. The names *Whight, Elderkin, Dyer,* and *Tete* were heard above the din of shrieks. A horrible cacophony of cries filled the region. Parson White believed this might be Judgment Day. He wasted no time in sounding the alarm. It was obvious the French and their Indian allies were on a murderous rampage in Old Windham.

By dawn, every man in town who owned a gun or a pitchfork assembled to march to the bloody scene and fight back against the invaders. Though the sounds of screams had grown more faint by sunrise, the mob could still follow the sounds toward Mullin Hill in the east part of town.

Just as the men from town crested Mullin Hill, they looked below and saw something awful. Thousands lay dead all around them. No one had ever witnessed anything like this before. The carnage was almost too gruesome to behold.

The previous afternoon's rain had created a small pond, or maybe more accurately a large puddle. As night fell, thousands of frogs descended on the puddle, making hideous shrieks and noises as they fought for the little water that was there. Those sounds, muffled by the distance and the trees, sounded human enough to freak out every person in Old Windham. By morning, many of the frogs were dead, and the men who came ready to fight had a good laugh in spite of themselves.

Locals wrote down the story in their journals and diaries, newspapers around the state reported the event as a great big joke, and, in 1891, a local newspaper man named N. W. Leavitt wrote down some words, and his son Burton Leavitt composed music for a comic opera titled *The Frogs of Windham*. The legend continued to grow over time. In 1924, the Daughters of the American Revolution placed a plaque to commemorate the event.

From there we . . . *err* . . . leap ahead to 1991 to Willimantic, the next town west of Windham. Willimantic had approved funding for a new bridge that would connect Route 32, across the train tracks and the Willimantic River, to Route 66 on South Street. Department of Transportation engineers proposed a design, but folks in town were not impressed. They wanted some style. Something interesting. The state caved and hired an architect—not something typically done for a bridge like this.

So at a cost of $13 million, the new bridge opened for business with adornments you don't see anywhere else in the state.

Willimantic used to be home to several cotton mills along the river that produced a lot of high-quality thread. The town was known as the thread capital of New England. So four pedestals were set at each corner of the bridge—those pedestals were made to look like spools of thread. Then you combine another local legend by adding eleven-foot-high frogs on the spools, and you have a bridge like no other with roots that run to places not even all the locals have heard about.

The Sleeping Giant

HAMDEN, CONNECTICUT

If you check out a topography map of Connecticut, you'll see that most of the hills and mountains run north and south. There are few exceptions, so when you do find one, you can't help but ask why . . . and how it got here.

Just behind Quinnipiac University in Hamden, Connecticut, sits one such mountain. The entire ridge is about one mile in length and its highest point sits 739 feet above sea level. Officially, it's called Mt. Carmel, though legend will tell you it's not a mountain at all.

Centuries ago, this region was home to the Quinnipiac people. The land was not only fertile, with abundant fresh water provided by the river, it also sat in a valley, which offered some protection from the weather. Then there's the abundant food offered by the ocean to the south. A number of important trade routes intersected here, allowing the Quinnipiac to trade and sometimes intermarry with other communities in the region. It was a great place to live, but there was only one problem . . . and it was a *big* problem: a giant deity named Hobbomock would wreak havoc on the region.

Hobbomock could be petulant. If he didn't get his way, he was known to stomp his feet, which had the power to redirect rivers and wipe out small villages. Wherever Hobbomock walked was a danger to the tiny humans at his feet. The giant would also scoop

up all the oysters he could find on the coast, leaving none for the Quinnipiac.

It's a problem living with a giant lurking around like that. That's when the creator-god Keitan stepped in to help the Quinnipiac people. Because Hobbomock was a divine creature, Keitan couldn't simply kill him. But when he saw the giant asleep there in the valley one day, Keitan seized the opportunity. The god cast a spell on Hobbomock, so the giant would sleep forever.

The spell worked, the giant slept, and peace returned to the region. As years passed, moss, then grasses, then trees began to grow over the sleeping giant until he was completely covered. Even today, this odd east-to-west hill is best known as the Sleeping Giant. When viewed from the right perspective, and when you know the backstory, it's easy to see why.

The Lordship Sea Serpent and Mermaid

STRATFORD, CONNECTICUT

From the shadow of Stratford Point's picturesque lighthouse comes the strange tale of a giant sea serpent, and later a mermaid, witnessed by none other than the lighthouse keeper at the time, Theodore "Theed" Judson.

Old Theed served as the lighthouse keeper from 1880 to 1920. Unlike other lighthouses, where the keeper and his family are stuck on an island, Stratford Point Lighthouse sits in the Lordship section of Stratford on the southern tip of a peninsula jutting into Long Island Sound. So, while the keeper must always tend to his duties, his family can utilize local schools, shopping, churches, and everything else available on the mainland.

Still, Theed took his job seriously as a keeper and an observer of the water. In July of 1886, Judson went on the record with the *Bridgeport Union* newspaper, describing the creature he saw. The beast was described as a sea serpent with pea-green whiskers, plowing through the water at a twenty-five-knot clip when he passed the Stratford lighthouse and left a wake of foam behind him a mile in length. Judson said the monster was easily two hundred feet in length, and his head reared twenty feet above the brine. That afforded a good look at his whiskers, which were the rich deep-green color of bog hay.

In addition to Theed Judson, other witnesses included his wife, his son Henry, his daughter Agnes, and H. W. Curtis of Stratford, as well as a number of people at Captain John Bond's place up the river.

"I saw it plainly," Judson said, "and so did my wife and children and Mr. Curtis. All of us are familiar with the appearance of a school of porpoises, and this sight was entirely different . . . It could be plainly seen without a glass."

A month later, none other than Connecticut native P. T. Barnum offered a $20,000 reward for the capture of a sea serpent dead or alive.

If witnessing one monster isn't enough, Old Theed had an even more fantastical sighting by the lighthouse eighteen

years later. This time, Judson said he saw and almost captured a mermaid. His account made the newspapers back in August of 1904.

Judson said, "I was busying myself about the place on Monday when I heard a voice, angelic, it seemed to me, and stranger than any songstress I had ever heard, coming from the vicinity of the point. I proceeded to investigate and from the bluff saw a mermaid seated on one of the rocks, her hair hanging in golden tresses down her back, and she [was] brushing it. I made up my mind to capture her, and in order to do so realized that strategy was necessary, so I made a circuit of the ground to the west and getting to the water's edge crept stealthily toward the rock.

"Unmindful of the approach of anyone, the angelic creature sung her love ditty and I am free to admit that no music I have ever heard so enchanted me. I dodged behind rock after rock, stopping from time to time, fearful lest she might hear my approach until at last all chance of seclusion for me was gone, and with one bound I made for the mermaid and seized her about the waist. With a scream she struck at me with her brush, landing on my forehead and knocking my cap into the water. Then, with a swish of her tail she caught me on the chin.

"Another instant, she had seized me by the hair. All this time I was struggling with her and had started for the shore, but when the prize was fairly within my grasp, she gave a wiggle, and slipped like an eel out of my arms, dove into the water, and with a tantalizing laugh, dove out of sight.

"This is a true mermaid story, and if you are inclined to doubt it, or anyone else, I have the hair brush that I picked up with my cap from the water to prove the truth of what I tell you."

The reporter noted that the hairbrush looked like any other hairbrush he'd ever seen. Judson offered the obvious explanation that mermaids get their hairbrushes from the staterooms of sunken ships.

At one time, decades earlier, P. T. Barnum had also offered a $20,000 reward for the capture of a mermaid. Whether that reward was still swimming in Judson's head, we'll never know.

Believe the lighthouse keeper or don't. *Lordship* knows he had his detractors. Some called him "Theed" Judson, others called him "Crazy" Judson. No matter what, he kept the watch for forty years and left us with some Long Island Sound legends to ponder.

The Nation's Most Controversial First Hamburger

NEW HAVEN, CONNECTICUT

Please don't shoot the messenger on this one. We know there are many places that claim they served the nation's first hamburger. While we won't go into all of the various claims, we will say our source on this is the restaurant that's still in operation in New Haven, *and* the United States Library of Congress . . . *boom*!

On Crown Street in downtown New Haven sits an icon called Louis's Lunch. Established in 1895, the restaurant's humble beginnings were in the form of a food wagon operated by a German immigrant named Louis Lassen. Louis's food wagon got its start selling butter and eggs; in 1895, he added some broilers to cook and sell some hot food items to busy workers in downtown New Haven who were looking for a quick lunch.

Lassen used vertical broilers that could cook both sides of the meat at once, so the food could be ready fast. The grease dripped to the bottom and customers got meat evenly cooked every time.

Lassen would chop the meats and trim the fat, but soon figured out that if he gathered up all of those trimmings he could squish them into a patty, decrease his waste, have another food item to sell, and increase his profits. Some customers even preferred the meat-trimmings patties.

As the story goes, one day one of Lassen's regulars was in a terrible hurry, but also plenty hungry. He had no time to sit with a plate of food. So, he asked Louis to "Slap a meatpuck between two planks and step on it!" Lassen toasted two pieces of bread, placed the cooked meat patty between them, and his customer left with a portable hot meal. Other customers who weren't in a

hurry saw the order and thought it looked delicious. They asked for the same thing. And Louis's hamburger sandwich was born.

Louis's lunch wagon added new vertical broilers in 1898. After making a few hundred of these hamburgers, he had the recipe and timing down. Eventually, Lassen moved his operation into a permanent building on Crown Street in New Haven. Though Lassen died in 1935, his family continued the burger business using the same broilers first used in 1898, and the same upgraded toasters, purchased in 1929. In the 1960s, the building

LOUIS LUNCH
EST. 1895
LOUIS

was lifted onto a truck and moved four blocks up Crown Street to where it sits today.

In the 1950s, Ken Lassen added the option of cheese for your burger, but otherwise you get the burger with sliced onion and sliced tomato or any combination of the three. Whatever you do, don't you dare ask for ketchup, mayo, mustard, or any other condiments. They're not allowed. We're not kidding. You want a New Haven original, you'll have it *their* way, not *your* way.

As for the official "first" status, that happened in the year 2000. US Representative Rosa DeLauro (D-Connecticut) pushed for legislation to officially recognize Louis Lassen as the creator of the hamburger. The Library of Congress recorded that Lassen had served America's first hamburger, and then the nationwide fighting began as to who was really first. The hubbub doesn't bother the folks at Louis's Lunch too much. You can argue over who was first—they'll tell you they're the best.

The UFO Crash at Bantam Lake

MORRIS, CONNECTICUT

Bantam Lake is Connecticut's largest natural lake. It sits in Litchfield County and is just under a thousand acres in size. It's pretty. At twenty-five feet maximum depth, it's not very deep either. If something large sank there, it shouldn't be hard to find. On April 10, 2012, Bantam Lake became the site of something potentially out of this world.

Around 2:00 a.m., a man driving near the lake saw something large, green, and glowing, falling from the sky. The driver reached for his cell phone to call 9-1-1 and report it. The driver described something as big as a whale falling into Bantam Lake.

Around this same time, a Connecticut state trooper ten miles away in Warren, Connecticut, called his dispatcher to say he'd just seen a glowing object falling out of the sky in the area of Bantam Lake in Morris, Connecticut.

Unsure of what it could be, law enforcement contacted the Federal Aviation Administration (FAA) to make sure all aircraft were accounted for. They were. By daylight, search and rescue took to the lake, looking for any sign of wreckage, but they too found nothing. The National Weather Service confirmed that there had been a meteor shower the previous night, but if a meteor the size of a whale made it through our atmosphere and impacted the Earth at roughly thirty thousand miles per hour . . . well . . . Connecticut would be a crater today.

So we're left with an unknown flying phenomenon observed by multiple witnesses as a glowing green object that descended in or on Bantam Lake in April of 2012. We're not saying it's aliens . . . but . . .

Yo Ho Ho and a Burial of Rum

LEBANON, CONNECTICUT

The grave marker of Captain Sluman Gray in Liberty Hill Cemetery in Lebanon, Connecticut, is unassuming. However, it's what's belowground that makes this grave unique. A few feet down there's a barrel of rum that Captain Gray was simply dying to get into.

In March of 1865, the whaling ship *James Maury* was sailing four hundred miles off the coast of Guam in the South Pacific. At the helm was Captain Sluman Gray, a tyrant of a leader who ruled with an iron fist. In the 1860s, the whaling trade was booming. Demand for whale oil was high, whale bones were sought after for other products, as was the blubber. Competition was fierce, and with all the whaling happening all over the world, supplies were running low. Whaling ships had to sail far from home to find the whales. And vessels like the *James Maury* didn't return home until their cargo holds were full, which could take years and span the globe.

Sailing with Captain Gray on this voyage was his wife, Sarah, and three of his children: Katie, who was sixteen, Sluman Jr., who was ten, and little Nellie, who was only two years old.

On March 22, their ship was sailing off the coast of Guam. Captain Gray fell ill, much to the delight of his crew who had some peace while the captain was laid up in his quarters with his wife tending to him. Illness at sea is always a concern, but Gray had pulled through things like this before.

But his wife suspected that this was different. With each passing hour his condition worsened. After only two days of being sick, Captain Gray died. The first mate entered the note in the ship's log.

A burial at sea is customary in these circumstances. No one wants a rotting corpse on board, potentially spreading a fatal illness. But the captain's widow wouldn't hear it. She insisted that her husband needed a proper burial back home in Connecticut. Against his better judgment, the ship's cooper made a barrel large enough to fit the captain inside. Once properly stuffed into the barrel, they filled the empty space with rum to preserve the body, and then they sealed up the barrel.

With the cargo hold not yet full of whale oil, bones, and blubber, the voyage continued for another year before the *James Maury* finally made it back to its home port of New Bedford, Massachusetts. The Widow Gray had her husband's rum barrel brought back to her home in Lebanon, Connecticut, where she was advised that opening that barrel after being sealed for a year could be quite gruesome. In the end, it was decided that the best course of action was to dig a grave and make the rum barrel his casket. Which is where the mortal remains of Captain Sluman Gray still lie pickled today . . . We'll drink to that.

Bank Street's Haunted Stove

NEW MILFORD, CONNECTICUT

Back in September of 1930, Hawk Palardy was working at a restaurant on Bank Street in New Milford, Connecticut. In the alley behind the restaurant was a shack that held an old stove, as well as sacks of potatoes, onions, and other food items that took up too much room in the kitchen. Palardy had been sent out to the shack to fetch some onions for the kitchen. As soon as he entered the shack, he heard a disembodied voice call out, "Hey, Hawk! Can you hear me?"

Startled by the voice with no source, and finding no living person nearby, Palardy dropped the onions and raced back inside, petrified. He relayed his experience to the kitchen staff who laughed at the poor guy. No one believed him . . . not yet.

The following evening the restaurant owner asked Palardy to head out to

NEW MILFORD PUZZLED BY GAS STOVE GHOST

New Milford, Sept. 7, (AP)—A talking ghost has taken up its residence in an old stove in a barn here, and draws hundreds of curious nightly.

The ghost, which started its talking about a week ago, has been taking part in the investigation of the disappearance of Kenneth Swanson, two-and-a-half year old Barre, Vt. boy missing from the home of his grandparents in Colebrook, for several weeks.

The voice, listeners say, is weak and often distorted. It seems to come from an old gas stove. Various theories have been put forward by those who don't believe in ghosts. Some say its just a clever ventriloquism stunt and others think the stove may be hooked up to a radio broadca[illegible]ing station.

the shack and peel potatoes for the restaurant. Palardy said he'd do it, but he was too afraid to go alone. So, a young kitchen assistant accompanied Palardy to the shack in the alley.

The two had just begun peeling potatoes when a disembodied voice called out, "Help! Help! I'm buried forty feet underground. Help! Help!"

After the kitchen assistant and Palardy raced back inside, shaking with fear, claiming they just heard a child's voice coming from the old stove in the shack, they found the staff no longer laughing. Soon, word spread as customers and other New Milford locals gathered in the alley near the stove in the shack. Most were incredulous. Even laughing. But then a woman bent down to listen by the stove. That's when many in the crowd heard a voice cry out, "Help! A young boy is buried in a cellar in Kent!"

Kent is a town about fifteen miles north of New Milford. Among the crowd was Harry Worley. His father owned the *New Milford Times* newspaper. Worley wrote up the story of the haunted stove and placed the article on the wire service. The news went viral. Dozens of newspapers all over the world ran the story. Within days, the crowds around Bank Street grew to thousands of people who wanted to hear the ghostly voices for themselves.

Given the public pressure, Kent police even conducted a search, looking for a child in a basement, but they found nothing, nor any reports of any missing children.

Priests arrived in New Milford to explore if this was a bona fide miracle. Skeptical police officers and detectives were among the crowd believing they could prove it was a hoax. Some local radio engineers were convinced the stove had somehow picked up radio signals and that explained the voices.

The streets were packed, and the voices continued coming from the stove with no explanation. One evening, forty men showed up, ready to conduct an all-night vigil if they had to. Around midnight, suddenly the lights in the alley dimmed, and then went out. Then a voice cried out from the stove, "Help meeeee!"

This continued into mid-October. The New Milford police had their hands full with crowd control alone. Crowd estimates reached three thousand people. That's when New Milford police stepped in and nailed the shack shut and closed off the alley. The crowds left, and the voice from the stove was never heard from again.

From 1930, we leap ahead forty years to a *Hartford Courant* newspaper article where some of the folks involved in the story back in 1930 explained what happened. It turns out there used to be a refrigerator in the old shack in the alley with a rubber tube that ran into the building as a conduit for the electrical wire. That first night when Hawk Palardy went out to fetch some onions for the kitchen, one of the chefs realized he needed something else from the shack. So he placed his mouth up to the open end of the tube in the kitchen and called out, "Hey, Hawk! Can you hear me?" What started as a prank exploded into a ghostly mystery that served as a publicity boon for the town and the restaurant the likes of which was never seen again.

They Only Moved the Headstones

NEW LONDON, CONNECTICUT

Williams Memorial Park in New London is picture-perfect with its manicured grass, tasteful landscaping, and walkways through shady trees. A perfect place for a stroll, a break, or a picnic. Today, you'd never guess that this was once all cemetery grounds. You'd never guess unless . . . *you know* . . . you took a shovel and started digging just about anywhere. Then you'd figure it out pretty quickly.

We've all seen the movie *Poltergeist*. The fancy new housing development was built over a cemetery. But they only moved the headstones, not the graves. And that's why this new house was profoundly haunted. But that would never happen in real life, right? RIGHT?!

Williams Memorial Park is a four-acre piece of land. The historic district was established in 1885. But before that, it was the site of the boneyard known as Second Burial Ground.

Second Burial Ground was established in 1793 when a woman named Mary Rice had the distinction of being the first interred. Back then, New London was much smaller, and the cemetery was on the outskirts of town. But over time the cemetery filled up, and the town sprawled outward.

In 1885, Charles Augustus Williams was the mayor of New London. He had a vision for his city. He knew that cities often have a public park in the center while the city grows outward and upward. As New London was expanding, he didn't think it was right for the center of town to feature a cemetery and a quarry, and Mayor Williams was willing to put his money where his mouth was.

The mayor personally guaranteed to cover the price tag for relocating all the bodies from Second Burial Ground to the newer Cedar Grove Cemetery on the outskirts of town. And he would pay to get the land graded into a public park afterward. He believed a park would draw in more investments and developers because no one wants their home or business right next to a cemetery.

A public notice was put forth that bodies were being moved from the burial grounds. There were 770 graves in all. If you had a loved one interred there, you had the option of having them moved to a different cemetery at your own expense, or the city would relocate the grave at Mayor Williams's expense.

The work took about a year. Kids watched and gawked as headstones and caskets left the ground to be moved about a mile away to Cedar Grove Cemetery. In the end, the project cost about $8,000 and resulted in a public park aptly named after the brain and financier of the project, Mayor Williams. But did they move all the bodies or just the headstones?

From here we jump ahead to December 21, 1946, to a story in the *New London Evening Day* newspaper, where someone asked the very same question. They had heard that the headstones had been moved, but not the bodies. All of this came about because some folks in New London wanted to repurpose Williams

Memorial Park to be the site of a new civic center. Many people opposed the construction project because they wanted to keep the place a public park. Besides, detractors reasoned, this park is still burial grounds!

Evidence of that came in the form of the 1938 hurricane that ravaged New England. The storm uprooted one of the trees in the park (we'll pause for your *Poltergeist* movie flashback here), and you guessed it: Some bones and caskets came to the surface.

Okay, maybe a few bodies were left behind near the trees, you may think. But the 1946 article quoted Frederic W. Mercer, the vice president of National Bank of Commerce in New London. He said he was a kid when the cemetery was being relocated. The article said, "It is his recollection that about 770 persons were buried in the Second Burial Ground, and he insists that no more than 70 bodies were ever removed, indicating that some 700 still remain."

Enjoy your picnic if you go there today. Just don't try to build a house in the park . . . or a civic center. If Hollywood taught us anything, it's that the new building would definitely be haunted.

The Shoebox Murder Mystery

WALLINGFORD, CONNECTICUT

The headline says it all: DEAD IN A SHOE BOX: HIDDEN AWAY IN THE WOODS NEAR WALLINGFORD. A murder most foul, mysterious, and unsolved since 1886.

On Sunday morning, August 8, 1886, Wallingford local Edward Terrill and his dog were walking down the road next to Parker Farm. Something excited Terrill's dog near the low-lying bushes beside the road. The man followed his dog to see what he'd found. That's when he saw a box about thirty inches long and twelve inches wide. A box designed to hold twelve pairs of shoes. The box had been scraped and gouged to remove any identifying labels. As best Terrill could figure, the box had fallen off a passing wagon and had been left behind. But when he opened the box, the smell struck him first. He saw something wrapped in tar paper. With the black paper removed, he found the torso of a man. The arms, legs, and head had been removed. The inside of the box was soaked with blood and guts.

Terrill raced into Wallingford to fetch the authorities, who quickly gathered the box and the human remains and brought them to town for examination. The medical examiner inspected what was left of the victim, but found no clues. With nothing identifying on the box, their hopes of solving this crime were slim.

Still, the story made its way through the Wallingford rumor mill. People were guessing as to who it could be.

Some thought it could be the body of Albert J. Cooley of Durham, Connecticut, which is the next town over to the east of Wallingford. They said Cooley stole $1,500 from the pension of a local slaughterhouse. He was known to have tattoos on both arms, a deformed foot, and a bad eye. So he would have been easily identifiable . . . you know . . . unless you cut off his appendages. Plus, someone working at a slaughterhouse would have the tools and the know-how to take off a man's legs, arms, and head, for sure.

DEAD IN A SHOE BOX.

Hidden Away in the Woods Near Wallingford.

No Clue to the Mystery of the Mutilated Human Trunk Tied in Paper.

The Decaying Corpse Scented Under the Leaves by a Dog.

NEW HAVEN, August 8.—There has possibly occurred in Wallingford a most brutal murder. The murderer, whoever he may be, must have been as cool and calculating as the Marchioness de Brinvilliers. Today some young workmen in the shops thought to vary the monotony of their confined lives at the work-bench by taking a stroll out into the country. They had a dog with them and he walked on ahead.

The men, Edward and Joseph Terrill and Joseph Samson, went on until they came to the Parker farm, distant about three miles from Wallingford village. By-and-by they were in the woods, and the dog at once notified them that there was something that he wanted explained right away. They followed his warning and found that there was half hidden under a clump of bushes, an ordinary soapbox lying

The only problem with the theory was that authorities were able to track down the still-living Cooley in Durham.

The next lead came from Yalesville, the town just north of Wallingford. A witness claimed he'd seen this specific box, with its specific gouge marks, near Young's Slaughterhouse. The idea floated was that the body may have been dead for two or three months. There was speculation that the victim was a German butcher, named Martin, who had been missing for more than two months, and perhaps one of his fellow butchers had a big problem with his coworker.

So police explored this Yalesville butcher disappearance. They heard there were arguments, that Martin was the rough sort, and maybe this could have been a self-defense killing. But if you killed in self-defense, why would you go to such great lengths to dismember the body? You'd tell police you were defending yourself. So that theory didn't hold up either.

Meanwhile, the medical examiner determined that the body belonged to a man between the ages of twenty and forty, who died between five and ten days before he was found by Edward Terrill—which also ruled out the butcher named Martin. A large quantity of arsenic was discovered in the man's stomach—meaning someone wanted this person seriously dead. Poisoned. Dismembered. Dispersed.

Then another theory began to circulate. There had been a rash of arson fires around Wallingford in the weeks leading up to the gruesome find. Some people believed this might have been one of the arsonists who was getting ready to rat out his cohorts. But this was based solely on the fact that there hadn't been a fire since the body was found. So maybe this rumor was giving the real arsonists something to think about.

Throughout August, the newspapers ran all kinds of unsubstantiated stories. Locals were nervous that a monster was out there and they could be next.

The police were ultimately able to trace the box to a shoe factory in Fall River, Massachusetts. The factory explained that they filled the box with shoes, then sent it to a wholesaler in Chicago who distributed the shoes to local retailers. One of the Chicago retailers put the shoes on their shelves for sale, then tossed the box behind the store, where it sat for months before a mysterious man showed up and offered to buy the box.

So then police believed that perhaps the victim was from Chicago. There was speculation that the victim was one of the instigators of the Haymarket Square Riot that took place on May 4, 1886. But traveling nine hundred miles by train and horse to dispose of a body seemed like a lot more trouble than it was worth. Nothing added up. Police chased a few more random leads that came in, but nothing ever panned out. They asked around about missing men aged twenty to forty, but also struck out. Eventually, the case turned cold, and remains unsolved to this day.

The Glawackus

GLASTONBURY, CONNECTICUT

Film director, producer, and writer Joel Coen once said, "We create monsters and then we can't control them." That's a quote they know to be true in Glastonbury, Connecticut, because in 1939, a monster captivated the region as it grew to epic proportions in the span of about a month.

It all began in early January of 1839, in the then-rural farming community of Glastonbury. Some farm animals were turning up attacked and mutilated. Farmers knew what kind of predators lurked in the region, and they knew what those attacks looked like, but something was different about these attacks. It didn't look like the work of a mountain lion, a coyote, a dog, or any other common animal.

That's when Nat A. Sestero, a young newspaper reporter for the *Hartford Times*, caught wind of the animal attacks and wrote up the story for the newspaper. After all, this was news. Locals needed to be aware that something was terrorizing area farms.

Pelton Ferry, a stringer for the competing *Hartford Courant* newspaper, saw the story and went digging for his own witnesses. Joseph Bonvouleir of Hartford said he was "positive it was a black, powerful beast. I shot at it Saturday morning with my double-barrel shotgun. The left barrel fired, but missed. The right barrel failed to discharge."

Mrs. Rhoda D. Herrick of Hartford claimed she saw, "A slinking animal on the New London Turnpike at Ten Curves. It was a

dark, tawny color. It was about three feet long and two feet tall with a cat-like head."

By the description, it sounded almost like a puma or a black panther, neither of which is indigenous to anywhere near New England. Perhaps some animal escaped from a menagerie or circus? Maybe. But in the span of days, the public grew hungry for more stories about this strange beast. The descriptions quickly evolved to a lion-like creature with a horn like a unicorn.

Local radio personality Lowell Thomas broadcasted that an unnamed Connecticut scientist had identified this beast and given this creature a name: the Glawackus, or *Monstrum Infandum, Gallonobacchus*.

Glawackus fever gripped the region. Hunting parties formed to try to bag the new animal. The *Hartford Courant* printed maps of where sightings occurred. Then advertisers jumped in to capitalize by mentioning the Glawackus in their ads.

Advertisers like Plasikowski Incorporated, a business that made clothing from animal pelts, wrote a headline that read:

> We will gladly take the Glawackus pelt
> and make a Glawackus coat or scarf
> at our regular rates!

Laurel Oil Company's ad said:

> Be ready for a quick get-away
> from the Glastonbury Glawackus by using
> Laurel Oil Esso gasoline and a new Atlas battery!

The Binee salons advertised:

> DON'T LOOK LIKE A GLAWACKUS! GET YOURSELF SOME PERMANENT WAVES FOR $2.95 TO $3.45

We can only guess that the price depended on how Glawackus-like your hair was at the time of service.

Mohican Market featured a tiny line at the top of their ad that read: WE CANNOT AGREE TO SUPPLY YOU WITH [in big, bold letters it said] GLAWACKUS STEAKS, then continued: THEY'D BE MUCH TOO TOUGH AND STRINGY TO PLEASE YOU. Instead, they'll sell you sirloin, cube, or round steak for 33 cents per pound.

By February, Glastonbury threw a Glawackus Ball, and all the while this creature's legend was growing and evolving by the day. Finally, the *Hartford Courant*'s assistant state editor, Frank King, came clean to say he was the person who came up with the name. It wasn't some scientist. He combined a few words: Glastonbury, Wacky, and Us. The Glawackus.

Was the creature finally shot and mounted? Did it move away? Was it captured? None of the above. Sightings of the strange, black, cat-like animal continued, but readers grew bored of the stories and the news cycle moved on. For all we know, the Glawackus is still out there somewhere.

The Black Dog of Meriden

MERIDEN, CONNECTICUT

There are black dog legends all over the world. If you see one out in the wild, it's said to be a harbinger of bad things, maybe even death. Meriden, Connecticut's version of the legend is no different.

Castle Craig sits on the Hanging Hills overlooking Hubbard Park below. If you take a stroll through the park—especially on a nice day—you're almost guaranteed to see a dog, maybe even a black dog, on a leash with its owners. But this legendary black dog is different.

Most of what we know about this story comes from a work of fiction by William H. C. Pynchon who wrote it up in a 1898 edition of *Connecticut Quarterly* magazine. Pynchon wrote:

> It was late in the spring of 1894 that I visited West Peak for the first time. I was then a student at Harvard, and my work in geology made it desirable for me to visit the locality. At that time I had heard nothing of the legend . . . Guiding myself by the maps which I had brought with me, I reached this road and there got out of the wagon to examine the vesicular lava of which there was a good outcrop at that point. I had been on my knees pounding away for dear life in my endeavor to get off a good cabinet specimen and had just gotten up to straighten my back, when I noticed trotting up the road a dog. I suppose he might have been called black, but it was the same degree of blackness that you see in an old black hat that has been soaked in the rain a good many times. His lineage was evidently uncertain . . .

> He seemed friendly, and when I drove on he insisted on following the wagon. So I let him go with me for the sake of his good company. We made a jolly trio—the rough, strong old horse, the faded dog, and the man whose appearance was not one whit better than that of his companions . . .
>
> I took a great liking to that dog. In the first place he was so quiet. Not once in all that day did I hear him bark, even when a calf beside the road tried to coax him into a fight. And he was so light of foot! Though the roads were very dry, yet I did not see a puff of dust rise from his feet as he trotted along ahead of the horse.

Pynchon tells of how he never quite got the Hanging Hills of Meriden out of his head. Three years after his first visit, in the month of February, he returned to the region to find it under a blanket of snow. He hoped that with the grass and moss dead from the cold, more rocks would be exposed for his study. Pynchon spent the evening before the expedition in a local hotel with his friend, Herbert Marshall from the United States Geological Survey, who had climbed and surveyed West Peak many times in the past. The two talked by the fireplace until it was only embers. Marshall told Pynchon about the legend of the black dog, a dog Marshall claimed he'd seen twice before on previous trips to Meriden. The following morning, Marshall decided to accompany Pynchon on his trip back to the Hanging Hills. The two reached the peak around 11 a.m. Pynchon wrote:

> Marshall was in the lead, and I was following as best I could, when he suddenly stopped and without a word pointed to the top of the cliff. There, high on the rocks above us, stood a black dog like the one I had seen three years before, except that he looked jet black against the snow wreath above him. As we looked he raised his head and we saw his breath rise steaming from his jaws, but no sound came through the biting air. Once, and only once, he gazed down on us with gleaming eyes and then he bounded back out of sight. I looked at Marshall. His face was white and he steadied himself against a rock, but there was not a tremor in his voice as he said, "I did not believe it before. I believe it now; and it is the third time."
>
> And then, even as he spoke, the fragment of rock on which he stood slipped. There was a cry, a rattle of other fragments falling—and I stood alone.
>
> Later—I cannot tell how much later—there is no measure of hours and minutes at such a time—bruised, bleeding, almost frozen, I stood by all that was left of my friend. He was dead; his body was already stiff, and I knew that unless I would share this, his last sleep, I must hasten. So I bent over him in a hasty farewell and then staggered on.

Pynchon summed up the black dog legend: If a man shall meet the Black Dog once it shall be for joy; and if twice, it shall be for sorrow; and the third time he shall die.

Though a work of fiction, some believe the author based it on a true account he'd heard in the region. Black dog sightings have continued ever since. If you spot one there, pray you don't see him two more times.

The Ghost Ship of New Haven Harbor

NEW HAVEN, CONNECTICUT

In 1702, Cotton Mather (of the 1692 Salem witch trials fame) was one of the most influential religious figures of his time. He was on a mission to spread his religious ideas and ideals to as many people as possible. In that year, Mather published a book called *Magnalia Christi Americana*, which was a history of early New England's religious development. While working on his book, Mather had heard stories about a ghostly ship that was seen in New Haven Harbor, so he wrote a letter to Reverend James Pierpont of New Haven, asking for an account of the story. Reverend Pierpont, wrote him back:

> In compliance with your desires, I now give you the Relation of that Apparition of a Ship in the Air, which I have received from the most credible, judicious and curious surviving observers of it.
>
> In the year 1647, besides much other lading, a far more rich treasure of passengers (five or six of which were persons of chief note and worth in New Haven) put themselves on board a New Ship, built at Rhode Island, of about 150 tons, but so walty, that the master [Lamberton] often said she would prove their grave.

Walty means that the ship wasn't well constructed. She teetered and tottered in the water. The ship, called *New Ship* (the creative person who named vessels must have been out sick the day she was christened), was said to list to one side. Once tied to the docks in New Haven, she was loaded up with goods to be sold in England. This vessel was going to help establish New Haven as a significant seaport.

In January of 1647, the ship was ready to sail. However, the morning of embarkation offered a bad omen in the form of ice. So much ice had gathered on the decks and rigging that it needed to be chiseled off by the crew before she could set sail.

Reverend Pierpont's letter continued: "Mr. Davenport in prayer with and observable emphasis used these words: Lord, if it be thy pleasure to bury these our friends in the bottom of the sea, they are thine; save them!"

With that ominous blessing, *New Ship* left New Haven bound for England. A crowd of family, friends, and locals saw her off on that cold day until she sailed out of sight.

As days melted to weeks and no word of a sighting came from any other ships, the people of New Haven began to fret.

Reverend Pierpont wrote: "The Spring following no tidings of these friends arrived with the ships from England: New Haven's heart began to fail her. This put the Godly people on much prayer, both public and private, that the Lord would (if it was his pleasure) let them hear what he had done with their dear friends, and prepare them with a suitable submission to his Holy Will."

Now convinced that something awful had happened to the ship, the people of New Haven could only pray for answers or, at the very least, some closure. Their answer finally came with a literal message from above.

Reverend Pierpont said that by June, a great thunderstorm arose out of the northwest. An hour before sunset, the clouds formed into the shape of a ship that looked exactly like *New Ship*, which had sailed from their harbor and had never been seen again. There was the hull, the masts, the sails, and everything. This ghostly cloud ship sailed through the air toward land against the wind for close to half an hour.

Reverend Pierpont continued: "Many were drawn to behold this great work of God; yea, the very children cried out, There's a brave ship! At length, crowding up as far as there is usually water sufficient for such a vessel, and so near some of the spectators, as that they imagined a man might hurl a stone on board her, her main-top seemed to be blown off, but left hanging in the shrouds; then her mizzen-top; then all her masting seemed blown away by the board quickly after the hulk brought unto a careen, she overset, and so vanished into a smoky cloud, which in some time dissipated, leaving, as everywhere else, a clear air."

To the New Haven faithful, this was their answer as to the fate of their ship. It was lost in a storm. God literally showed them. And Cotton Mather took this ghostly tale as further evidence that God does indeed work wonders and does answer prayers (even if the answer to the prayer isn't the one you were hoping for).

Gungywamp

GROTON, CONNECTICUT

Gungywamp is an archeological, historic, and folkloric enigma. What we know for certain is that there have been millennia of human activity on this hundred-acre site dating as far back as possibly 2000 BC.

Gungywamp is the Pequot name for this hill and location. The name, like its stone structures, has survived the centuries.

Colonists lived here a few centuries ago—we can still see their cellar holes and foundations; Native Americans lived here because arrowheads and other artifacts have been found on the site. But a few of the other structures led some to speculate that the origins may even be European—all the way back to a time when Celtic people may have fled wars and turmoil in their own country.

What can't be denied is the strange feeling one gets when you follow the path by the nearby swamp into the darker forest where the ruins of this site sit waiting. Once you enter the former village, strange stone walls, covered in light-green lichen, run all over the complex. While seeing a stone wall in the woods of New England is nothing unusual, the layout of these walls is different. There's a sense that this was more than a village, that it's a sacred site.

One of the peculiar features of Gungywamp includes a stone cave in the hillside. At first glance, it appears to be a simple root cellar of some kind, but on closer inspection we see a small window in the back near the top. On the equinoxes, the sun shines

through that window and down to the lower corner where a smaller chamber has been carved out. So on two occasions each year (assuming it's a sunny day), that chamber is naturally illuminated by sunlight. European colonists didn't construct such things.

In the highest section of the site sit two rings of stone circles. It's believed that a giant ancient tree trunk sits below these stones, leading some to speculate that this was the heart, or most sacred part, of Gungywamp. Others suggest that these stones marked a colonial tanning mill where leather tanning took place. From here, one can observe the whole complex, ponder what happened, and connect with the layers of spirits and spirituality of those who came here long before us.

The Darn Man

HAMPTON, CONNECTICUT

The days of the vagabond are long past now, but there was a time when a special group of people were homeless by choice. They viewed true freedom as having no roots and no fixed address. To live this way required charisma, charm, personality, and some kind of schtick, because you needed to be interesting enough that folks wanted to talk to you. You had to be charming enough that they would invite you into their homes and offer you a meal or a bed for the night, and you needed to be memorable enough that they would recall you the next time you traveled through town.

The Darn Man or Old Darn Coat of Windham County, Connecticut, fit all those categories. The Darn Man's silhouette looked distinguished with his top hat and fancy dress coat, complete with tails, but when you got a closer look at him, you'd see that his coat was held together by strings of every conceivable color. It had been repaired and stitched so many times that you could hardly tell the coat's original shade. Whenever someone offered to stitch the coat for him, he'd insist on doing the work himself, but wouldn't mind the free thread for the sewing.

In 1920, Dr. A. D. Ayer wrote about his childhood recollections of the Darn Man visiting his family's Hampton home about once a month as he traveled from home to home around Windham County. He said whenever the lady of the house offered to do his mending, or replace his heavily stitched coat, he'd reply,

"These are my wedding clothes and they are sacred. My bride will be here soon." But no bride ever came.

Ayer recalled how very little was known about the Darn Man; he never seemed to give a straight answer to any question posed to him. He preferred to remain a mystery. Though locals must have trusted him enough to invite him in and feed him. Maybe people felt sorry for him because they believed that his bride had left him at the altar, and he'd been looking for her ever since.

Ayer documented something the Darn Man told him when Ayer was still young: "Boy, as you grow up, beware of the girls. Don't spend your money on them. Don't pay out for a nice wedding suit, especially a coat, for you may be left as I was, to wander about with my wedding coat I avowed to wear until I learned what became of the one whom I adored, who I am not willing to say went back on me. I am charitable enough to think she was spirited away, or lost her mind, and perhaps was killed . . . I have my mind made up to keep on going over the same route, in the same towns, and I expect to die some time in some of the places I have been for years."

In 1863, a farmer driving his wagon along Snake Meadow Hill Road in Sterling, Connecticut, discovered the Darn Man lying near the road. The farmer tried to get the old man help, but the Darn Man died in the wagon. He was buried in the Oneco section of Sterling. They say he was buried in his famous coat.

The Haunted Piano of Gardner Lake

SALEM, CONNECTICUT

Gardner Lake in Salem is just over five hundred acres in size with an average depth of eighteen feet. It's not the largest in the state, but it's a pretty spot, and according to legend, it's quite haunted. Those paddling along the lake, or even fishing along the shores, will report hearing the faint sounds of a piano playing, though no source can be found.

This haunted piano has its own backstory rooted in some odd history.

The winter of 1895 was brutal in this region of Connecticut. By mid-February it was reported that the ice on the Thames River just above the railroad bridge was already ten inches thick, the harbor drawbridge was frozen shut, and the mercury was hovering around ten below zero day after day.

While that bitter cold is uncomfortable for most people, there is an upside. Enter Thomas Lecount. Lecount was a wealthy grocer in Niantic who owned a handsome two-and-a-half story home on the south shore of Gardner Lake. Lecount also owned land on the eastern shore of the lake—a spot he thought was better suited for his home. So he hired a contractor to relocate the house from the southern shore to his land on the eastern shore.

Moving a house is an intricate and expensive endeavor. To move it by wagons on the road would be extremely difficult and risky, but the contractor had an idea. With the lake frozen solid, the house could be placed on skids and dragged across the lake

to the other side with no concern over roads, trees, or any other obstacles. *What could possibly go wrong?*

On February 10, 1895, a crew of men shoveled a path across Gardner Lake, while more workers lifted and jacked up the house onto giant wooden skids that would serve to move Lecount's home from its foundation and start it on its relatively short half-mile journey across the lake. Once that was complete, the process would repeat for Lecount's barn and bathhouse. So three buildings in total were going to make their way across Gardner Lake.

Because the process was going to be so smooth and easy, no items were removed from the house. The furniture, the carpets, the grand piano, the stove, even knickknacks on the shelves were left in place, because this was going to be so slow and easy there was no need to pack anything up.

The contractor estimated the house weighed about twenty-eight tons. The lake's thick ice sheet should be more than enough to handle it. And they were correct. The ice could handle twenty-eight tons of house on skids . . . *normally*.

On February 11, they began the work. At first the process was going smoothly. The house was raised, placed on skids, and then dragged onto the lake for its half-mile journey. But once they had pulled the house about 250 feet from shore, they heard some cracks and soon the house could go no further. More muscle was needed. It was decided to leave the house there overnight and recruit more horses the following day to finish towing the home.

When the crew arrived the following day, they saw that something awful had happened. The ice had cracked, and the heaviest part of the house—the side with the stove, chimney, and kitchen—had sunk a few feet into the broken ice. No matter how many horses they brought to help, the house wouldn't budge in any direction. That's when the contractors realized the horrible thing that happened. The night before, Falls Mill in Norwich, who owned the water rights to the lake, had no idea there was a house sitting on the ice when they decided to open their dam that night and drain a significant amount of water, creating a gap between the ice and the water level. The ice on the water could have handled the load of the house. Ice over air could not.

It was obvious to all that this house would be a total loss. They were able to remove most of the furniture and personal items, but a few things in the house were simply too heavy. Items like the stove and the grand piano.

For the rest of the winter, the sinking house was a spectacle to be seen by everyone who lived around the lake. Ice skaters skated up to and around Lecount's former home, and then spring's thaw eventually came, the ice melted, and the house mostly sank, though not entirely. It seemed to bob in the water while the lake slowly ate away at the wood and nails.

Each year there was less to see of the house until it was finally gone. Just a memory, and a postcard. But . . . they say you can still hear that old piano playing on the wind. A reminder of the time a house almost crossed Gardner Lake.

Massachusetts

Born: February 6, 1788

If Massachusetts had filed the paperwork a month earlier, maybe we would have been talking about New England's only commonwealth first instead of Connecticut. But alas, the Bay State does things on its own time and following its own agenda.

They start revolutionary wars when they're damn good and ready—like when those first shots were fired at Lexington and Concord (each town claims to be the site of the first shot, so it's best to list them both or it will start a fight). They throw tea parties like none the world has ever seen—a kettle in Beantown still steams to remind locals of their unique relationship with tea. The eastern half of the state talks different than most folks—a phenomenon called non-rhoticity where they drop the Rs (go ahead and say to a stranger in Boston, "Tell the gahdenah to pahk the cah in Hahvahd Yahd," and watch yourself get punched).

Then there's the western portion of the state where they hit those hard Rs like a punching bag out of protest. Boston politicians don't take much notice of Western Mass, and folks out there take it personally to the point of pulling colossal pranks on the legislature.

Massachusetts offers us unsolved murders and the nursery rhyme and haunting that followed, protests of all stripes and sorts, witches and devils, morons and geniuses, and though many outsiders call them Massholes, people in the Bay State have taken to wearing the label (and bumper sticker) with pride.

The Westford Knight

WESTFORD, MASSACHUSETTS

Stories of knights often conjure up images of medieval Europe with its castles, lords, ladies, and armor-clad warriors. *Old* England? Sure. But Massachusetts? Maybe.

Westford is a suburban town located just outside the I-495 loop. Driving through its Main Street you'll find nice homes, well-maintained, and spaced far enough apart for manicured lawns and gardens. However, just off the side of Depot Street sits a monument that looks out of place at first glance (and second glance, for that matter). Lying on a stone slab is the bronze statue of a medieval knight. Why he's there is a mystery that might date back as far as the year 1399 with ties to the Holy Grail.

The statue is a three-dimensional representation of a faded carving made into the rock just beside the statue. A carving first discovered in the year 1873.

In the 1930s, someone suggested that the carving had Irish origins. Not necessarily centuries old, but it could go back decades or even a hundred years to a time where there were already plenty of colonists here. But then in 1950, the theory was put forth that maybe this stone was a sign from Prince Henry Sinclair of Scotland's expedition to North America.

Back in 1390, Henry Sinclair commanded a fleet of thirteen warships with the goal of conquering Shetland, an island off Scotland (currently part of the UK), for King Hakon. After leaving victorious, he sailed home to Orkney, another island off Scotland. And that's when a fisherman who had been missing for twenty years started talking about a strange land full of native people. He said the land was temperate and beautiful. People in Scotland already knew about Greenland. But the fisherman insisted this land was much farther west.

In the fall of 1398, Sinclair and some of his knights sailed west. They passed Greenland and continued sailing until they found land. But this was not the temperate land he had heard about. This region looked more like Greenland's climate. Sinclair made camp for the winter and waited for spring's thaw. When the weather broke, Sinclair set his ship heading south and followed the coast of this newfound land.

After weeks of sailing, he found warmer temperatures and a greener environment than what he'd seen up north. After making landfall, Sinclair and some of his knights headed inland to explore. For weeks they studied this lush new world. All was well, until one of Sinclair's Knights Templar, Sir James Gunn, took ill and then died. Sinclair demanded the most fitting burial they could muster under the circumstances. His men obliged.

The next big question is this: Could this site in modern-day Westford have been the place where Sir James Gunn was buried and his likeness was carved into a rock, or could this be colonial graffiti, or some other carving?

To add more intrigue to the mystery, some believed there was a connection between the Knights Templar and the Holy Grail, so the next step in diving down this rabbit hole is to wonder if the grail was brought to America on this voyage.

One other piece of evidence surfaced in 1930 during construction of a road in Westford. A carved rock, now called the "Ship Stone," depicts a crude carving of a sailing ship on a small boulder with an arrow pointing up. It's speculated that this rock marked the way to Sinclair's ship.

The "Ship Stone" is now on display in the J. V. Fletcher Library in Westford. And the monument to the Westford Knight has only grown in size and legend with the passage of time. While seeing the ancient carving of the knight in the rock requires some imagination today, the bronze statue beside it does not. Now . . . if we could just find that grail . . .

Forklore on Old Harbor Road

WESTPORT, MASSACHUSETTS

If you head south on Old Harbor Road in Westport, when you reach the fork in the road . . . you've arrived. You can't miss it.

The fork's creator, Tom Schmitt, drove by this intersection almost every day for years. He has a sense of humor that—lucky for us—is prone to puns. "It's the quintessential fork in the road," Schmitt told us.

Now retired, Schmitt spends a lot of his time in his shop working on boats. One day back in 2010, while he was visiting his favorite lumberyard, he saw some mammoth slabs of pine that he thought would be perfect for the project that had been swirling in his head for years. The price was cheap, so he loaded the wood into his truck and took it home.

He grabbed a fork from his kitchen drawer and some calipers, and began scaling up his design. He did the rough work with a chain saw, the finer work with power tools and sandpaper. He sealed it, painted it, and had a fork standing roughly twelve feet tall.

The night before Memorial Day 2010, Schmitt and his wife lugged his creation to the intersection between Old Harbor and River Roads and attached it to a stone pillar that has been there since horse-and-buggy days. After only a minor delay from a passing police officer who shined his police light at the couple to ask what they were doing, then left with a smile on his face, the fork . . . in the road . . . was erected.

After a good laugh himself, Schmitt and his wife left the fork for all to enjoy . . . which lasted about twenty-four hours, because something that funny is going to get stolen. After a day, the fork turned up attached to one of the pilings on the wharf at the harbor entrance in town. A fine prank, but not the location Schmitt envisioned for his art. I mean, no one has heard of a fork in the wharf, right?

Schmitt recovered the fork and brought it home. He needed to up his foundation game, so he attached his wooden fork to a metal pipe and secured it into the ground with rocks and dirt. This time the fork lasted until the following summer when someone figured out that if they wiggled the sculpture back and forth long enough, it would get loose. The oversized utensil was later found wedged into a fractured rock at the local beach club—as if stuffed there by some giant, fresh off his beanstalk descent.

This forked-up incident forced Schmitt to further escalate his efforts for roadside-oddity permanence. On a Saturday morning, he invited a bunch of friends to each bring a sack of concrete and come to a digging party. This time the crowd helped dig a hole deep and wide, and mixed enough cement to fill the new hole with roughly a ton of steel-reinforced concrete. And there the fork has stood ever since.

Once a year, Schmitt polishes up the fork with fresh paint, and on July Fourth and Labor Day, he's been known to place a hot dog atop the tines. But . . . as all good legends do . . . the forklore spread. Couples getting married have placed wedding veils on top for the photo opportunity, a giant Santa hat has been placed there

at Christmastime, even a meatball and pasta made from papier mâché has been seen gracing this mighty fork.

But not everyone likes it, Schmitt explained. Every town has its complainers, and Westport is no different. "A fork like this would never appear in the Hamptons," one local wrote in the newspaper's letters to the editor section.

"But the backlash from the people who were friends of the fork was gratifying," Schmitt said. It would seem Westport is mostly okay with not being the Hamptons, thank you very much.

How does one get permission to put up a new landmark? You could go through the town and hope to pass through a significant maze of elected officials and town meeting bureaucracy . . . or just ask the landowner and leave it at that. Schmitt chose the latter.

"As many of my friends tell me, I have too much time on my hands," he said. But there's some pride in his voice when he tells of being labeled the Fork Guy.

We all want to leave a mark.

"That wasn't my point at the time," Schmitt said, "but it has become a landmark. People chuckle when they drive by. It achieved what I wanted people to see. And it gives you the opportunity to not take yourself too seriously."

Lizzie Borden Took an Axe

FALL RIVER, MASSACHUSETTS

Lizzie Borden took an axe
And gave her mother forty whacks.
When she saw what she had done
She gave her father forty-one.

What New Englander could forget the childhood rhyme of Lizzie Borden's most horrible deed?

Unsolved murders shake entire communities to their foundations. Even when those murders occurred over a century ago, we're haunted by the evil act. On August 4, 1892, an assailant entered 92 Second Street in Fall River, and murdered Andrew and Abby Borden with a hatchet. Both victims were brutally bludgeoned, there was no sign of forced entry, nothing stolen, and no sign of a struggle . . . these victims knew their killer.

All signs pointed to Andrew's daughter, Lizzie, and she was soon arrested. What followed was the trial of the century. Despite all circumstantial evidence leading to Lizzie as the murderer, a year later she was acquitted and lived the rest of her life a free, yet notorious woman.

Today, the Lizzie Borden Bed-and-Breakfast looks much as it did back in 1892. But the décor isn't the only echo from the past. This home is one of New England's most active haunts. Guests have fled in the middle of the night after witnessing dark shadows lurking in the guest rooms. One small group touring the house

Lizzie
Borden
bed & breakfast
NO VACANCY
c. 1845

watched as a picture frame floated into the middle of the front parlor, then flipped over onto the floor. An overnight guest went to sleep in Bridget Bishop's Room—the living quarters of the Bordens' former maid. The guest woke up to find the rocking chair had moved to right next to the bed as if some specter had been watching her as she slept.

Running phantom footfalls, whispering voices, and shadows from the past still haunt the iconic home today. No matter what you choose to believe (or not believe), a double unsolved murder will haunt us for as long as we continue talking about the crime.

Persecuted for Wearing a Beard

LEOMINSTER, MASSACHUSETTS

Today's hipsters wouldn't have lasted five minutes in 1830s New England. Though not illegal, beards on men weren't just frowned upon, they could get you shunned, attacked, and maybe even killed. Joseph Palmer would know!

When you stroll through Evergreen Cemetery in Leominster, you can't miss the monument with Joseph Palmer's embossed and heavily bearded smirking face staring at you. He looks almost like Santa Claus without the hat. And there's the name PALMER at the bottom, but it's the inscription just below the face that begs the biggest question: PERSECUTED FOR WEARING THE BEARD.

What?!

Joseph Palmer was born in 1789. A deeply religious Christian man, Palmer began growing his whiskers in the 1820s. His goal was to emulate the biblical figures he so admired: Jesus, Noah, Moses, and others who all wore beards. While that may be true, Palmer's minister didn't like it one bit. By 1830, his minister suggested (read: commanded) a shave. When Palmer refused, his minister accused him of being in league with Satan.

One day, while making a delivery to the Fitchburg Hotel, Palmer was jumped by four men. While holding him down, one of the men tried to cut off Palmer's beard. In the scuffle, Palmer pulled a pocketknife from his coat and stabbed at his attackers. When police arrived, they took one look at Palmer . . . or rather, his beard . . . and arrested *him*.

While sitting in Worcester County Jail for months, Palmer wrote letters to area newspapers, eloquently explaining his plight, and highlighting the deplorable conditions in jail. Soon, public outcry turned in his favor and the authorities were forced to let him walk free.

The reason for all of the anti-beard sentiment came down to one thing: That's what Jewish men do, *not us*. So good old-fashioned antisemitism was the reason for the persecution.

By the time Palmer died in 1873, beards were quite in fashion—check out just about any Civil War officer's portrait, or President Lincoln's mug, for that matter. Yet, Palmer never forgot how he was treated in his younger days just for sporting facial hair. His final gesture in life was to erect a monument to a man scorned for wearing a beard.

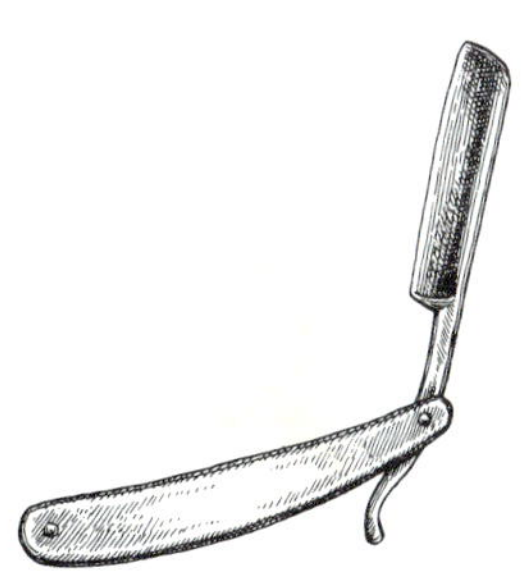

The Great Molasses Flood

BOSTON, MASSACHUSETTS

In the annals of Beantown history, few catastrophes can match that of the Great Molasses Flood of 1919 that left 21 dead and 150 injured.

Picture this: It was January 15, 1919, at the site of the Purity Distilling Company in Boston's North End. Molasses was a vital commodity back then. You could distill it to make rum for drinking, ethanol for fuel, and it was also used in making industrial alcohol for munitions. Two months before this disaster, the World War I combatants reached an armistice in Europe. So this factory had been running at full capacity for years to keep up with global demand.

That high demand was part of the problem. Corners were cut. A giant storage tank was quickly assembled less than four years earlier during the height of World War I. It was fifty feet tall, ninety feet across, and painted bright blue. It was capable of holding 2.5 million gallons of molasses.

With the tank full, workers noticed some of the brown molasses dripping from a few weak seams. Workers would place jars under the leaks to collect and bring the molasses home to their own kitchens. Instead of fixing the seams or building a new tank, the company decided to paint the tank the same brown color as the molasses to hide the leaks.

In the days leading up to January 15, it had been bitterly cold in Boston. Molasses doesn't freeze due to its high sugar content, but the low temperatures did help to hold the filled-to-capacity tank together. On January 15, there was a break in the cold snap. Temperatures rose into the forties. Cold contracts. Heat expands.

Just after noon on Wednesday, January 15, witnesses described what sounded like gunfire coming from the area. What they heard were rivets from this massive tank firing off like bullets moments before the steel sides ripped open, spilling 26 million pounds of molasses and sending it flooding down Commercial Street in Boston.

The wave of molasses was fifteen feet high, and moving at an estimated speed of thirty-five miles per hour. Buildings in the path of the wave were ripped from their foundations, and the molasses snapped the steel support girders from the elevated train track like dry twigs. Anyone caught in the path of the wave didn't stand a chance. You can't run thirty-five miles per hour.

Twenty-one people were either crushed by the wave and its debris, or they drowned in the brown, sticky goo. The wave created a half-mile path of destruction in Boston.

Police and rescue crews arrived quickly, but there was only so much that could be done. The aftermath was devastating. Beyond the human toll, there was an estimated $100 million in damages in today's dollars. The molasses poured into drainage systems and was tracked all over the city via people's shoes. The whole thing was a sticky, deadly mess of a catastrophe.

22 Pages Today

The Boston Post

EXTRA

THURSDAY, JANUARY 16, 1919

HUGE MOLASSES TANK EXPLODES IN NORTH END; 11 DEAD, 50 HURT

Giant Wave of 2,300,000 Gallons of Molasses, 50 Feet High, Sweeps Everything Before It—100 Men, Women and Children Caught in Sticky Stream—Buildings, Vehicles and L Structure Crushed

35 STATES ON DRY LAW LIST

Amendment Ratified by Five Yesterday—One More Needed—Predict Nation Dry July 1

SECRECY IN PEACE CONGRESS

France, Italy and Japan Outvote U. S. and Britain

BOY'S STORY AID TO MRS. LEBAUDY

Messenger Left Mansion Before the Shooting—Life in Danger

Search for More Victims During the Night

No Escape From Gigantic Wave of Fluid

INTERNAL EXPLOSION WAS CAUSE, SAYS STATE CHEMIST

A 50-foot wave of molasses—2,300,000 gallons of it—released in some manner yet unexplained, from a giant tank, swept over Commercial street and its waterfront from Charter street to the southerly end of North End Park yesterday afternoon.

Ensnaring in its sticky flood more than 100 men, women and children; crushing buildings, teams, automobiles and street cars—everything in its path—the black, reeking mass slapped against the side of the buildings topping Copp's Hill and then swished back towards the harbor.

Eleven persons—a woman, a girl and nine men—were the known dead at midnight. More than 50 injured were in hospitals and at their homes. Some of them may die. Dead horses, cats and dogs had been carted away in team after team.

Boston's only trolley freight terminal was in ruins. Most of its big steel trolley-freight cars were destroyed.

News of North End disaster on pages 5, 14, 15 and 16

KNOWN DEAD

MRS. BRIDGET CLOUGHERTY, 6 Copp's Hill terrace, North End.

WILLIAM A. DUFFEY, 67 Brighton street, West End.

ENGINEER GEORGE LAHEY, Engine 31, B. F. D., 401 Saratoga street, East Boston.

JAMES LENNON, 87 Brook avenue, Roxbury. Employee Public Works Department.

JOHN SEIBERLICH, 23 Fulda street, Roxbury. Employee Public Works Department.

PETER FRANCIS, 45 Monument street, Charlestown, employee Public Works Department.

JAMES J. KENNEALLY, 260 Bolton street, South Boston, employee Public Works Department.

THOMAS NOONAN.

MICHAEL SINNOTT, 78, 70 Bernard street, Dorchester.

WILLIAM BROGAN, 187 Webster street, East Boston.

UNIDENTIFIED DEAD

Girl about 14 years of age. She wore a gray jacket over a woolen middy blouse and carried a bag with an employment tag of the Revere Rubber Company.

SERIOUSLY INJURED

JOHN J. NOONE, 49, 41 Lawrence street, Charlestown. Employee Public Works Department. Fractured skull, fractures both legs. City Hospital; dangerous list.

ANTONIO DI STAZIO, 118 Charter street, North End. Compound fracture of skull. City Hospital; dangerous list.

OWEN GORMAN, 35 Tremont street, Charlestown. Employee Public Works Department. Injuries to chest, nose, left eye and fractures both legs. Haymarket Relief Station.

INJURED

JOSEPH BARRY, 9 Pine street, South End. City Hospital.

SAMUEL BLAIR, 4 Anderson street, West End. Haymarket Relief Station.

CHARLES BOWER, U. S. S. Starling, Navy Yard, Charlestown.

NATHANIEL BOWERING, Engine 31, B. F. D., 68 Decatur street, Charlestown.

PATRICK BREEN, 45 Fayette street, South End. Employee Public Works Department. Haymarket Relief Station.

CHARLES J. CASEY, 27 Dacia street, Roxbury. City Hospital.

CHILDREN NEED

L. C. COUGH DROPS

Real After-the-War News

BOSTON TAVERN

347 Washington Street 347

Interest Begins JAN. 18 — $4\frac{1}{2}$% Last Two Dividends $4\frac{1}{2}$% — BLACKSTONE SAVINGS BANK

DINE AT HEALY'S — 60c

HENRY F. MILLER & SONS PIANO CO. — FINE PIANOS — 395 BOYLSTON STREET

SHORTHAND

COUNTRY HOME

CASTLE SQ. THEATRE

Every $20 Overcoat $14

QUINCY HOUSE — 400 ROOMS—$1.50 A DAY — Broiled LAMB CHOPS — 70c — PLANKED STEAK $2.50

Interest Begins Jan. 23 — RECENT DIVIDENDS At the Rate of $4\frac{1}{2}$% — CAMBRIDGE SAVINGS BANK

$10 Young Men's O'Coats $5

Every $40 Overcoat $25

DREYFUS — Est. 1892 — SPECIAL ANNOUNCEMENT — TODAY'S MENU 45c — French Table d'Hote de Luxe, 5:30 to 8:30 P. M., $1.00

FAIR

HIGH TIDE TODAY — SUN — MOON

Every $15 Overcoat $7.90

Pants at a Price

FORD OWNERS DON'T CRANK IN VAIN

CLARK'S HOTEL

Witch Bonney Awaits

LOWELL, MASSACHUSETTS

Massachusetts is no stranger to witches, spells, and curses, and, of course, New England is no stranger to gravestones and monuments to the dead that take on a life of their own. In Lowell Cemetery, one monument more than any other commands your attention. The sight alone will cause a shiver to race up your spine as you view the feminine figure with outstretched arms holding a cloak as if she'd just leapt from a tomb behind her. This is a figure locals call Witch Bonney.

A closer look at the statue reveals that she's wearing a toga-like dress, barely clinging to her upper torso. One legend claims that the closer the calendar draws to Halloween, the more cleavage the statue reveals, until November comes around again, and Bonney takes on a more modest appearance.

Draw even closer, and you'll see the finer details of her face. Her hollow eyes gaze off into eternity. The black streaks below her eyes are said to be dark and angry tears.

Witch Bonney commands your respect. Should her grave be mocked, or if her memory should be snickered at, a powerful curse is said to befall the offender.

Here's what we know: The statue was erected in memory of Clara Bonney Lilley, who died from consumption on July 19, 1894 at age thirty-nine. Clara had recently welcomed her first child into the world, and the task of motherhood was more than her weakened state could handle.

Clara's father, Arthur, must have believed a curse was hanging over his family, because a year and a half earlier, he had just buried his wife, who also died from tuberculosis. And now he was forced to lay his only child into the same family plot. Arthur didn't linger very long after Clara's death. Less than two years after Clara passed, he spiraled into a deep depression and died officially from "unknown causes," but his friends would say the real culprit was a broken heart.

Perhaps Bonney isn't so much a witch, but a spirit who left behind the most unfinished business one could ever leave: raising her child. Maybe those dark tears are for the life she would have given anything to live. And maybe it's a good idea not to mock the memory of a person who has already suffered so much . . . it could make her even more angry.

The Sea Serpent of Gloucester and Rockport

GLOUCESTER AND ROCKPORT, MASSACHUSETTS

Stories of giant serpents have graced the shores of New England (and some of our largest lakes) for centuries. No matter how many witnesses, no matter how much ink these colossal beasts receive in the press, some still doubt their existence. "I need to see it to believe it" is a common response to extraordinary claims. However, some skeptics hear a claim so many times that they decide it's time for them to investigate first-hand to settle the matter. Annnnd . . . the newspapers publish yet another story on the Sea Serpent of Gloucester and Rockport.

The beast has been described as over one hundred feet in length and as large around as a barrel. The earliest account we could find dates back to 1638: "At this time we had some neighbouring gentlemen in our house, who came to welcome me into the country; where amongst variety of discourse, they told me . . . of a seas-serpent or snake, that lay quoiled up like a cable upon a rock at Cape Ann: a boat passing by with English aboard, and two Indians disswaded them, saying, that if he were not kill'd out-right, they would be all in danger of their lives," John Josselyn reported on June 26, 1638. His account was later published in his book, *An Account of Two Voyages to New England.*

This July 26, 1886 (248 years later, if you're keeping score) *Boston Globe* article is just one of many on the infamous monster.

The very reliable sea serpent has visited the scene of the coming harbor of refuge, Rockport breakwater. This is no imaginary sea serpent existing in the fertile mind of an enthusiastic newspaper man or concocted for the benefit of any particular watering place. This serpent is vouched for by men of undoubted veracity. Charles A. Russell, Esq., of Gloucester;

FISHY, BUT OFFICIA

Big as a Barrel and 1

Feet Long.

Gloucester Men See the Sea Serpent at the Breakwater.

They Are Sceptical No Longer About the Monster.

ROCKPORT, July 26.—The very reliable sea serpent has visited the scene of the coming harbor of refuge, Rockport breakwater. This is no imaginary sea serpent, existing in the fertile mind of an enthusiastic newspaper man, or concocted for the benefit of any particular watering place. This serpent is vouched for by men of undoubted veracity. Charles A. Russell, Esq., of Gloucester, lawyer Edward Battis of Salem, Sumner D. York, clerk of the Gloucester Police Court, and Albert W. Tarr, teller in the Rockport National Bank, have been camping out at what is known as Gully point. Saturday evening Mr. Tarr sat with glas in hand and saw a large body not fa shore. It was a monster. The the rest of the party large body. Ever were unbeliev but ocular doubt lawyer Edward Battis of Salem; Sumner D. York, clerk of the Gloucester Police Court; and Albert W. Tarr, teller in the Rockport National Bank, have been camping out at what is known as Gully Point. Saturday evening Mr. Tarr sat with glass in hand and saw a large body not far from shore. It was a monster. The attention of the rest of the party was called to the large body. Every one of the party were unbelievers in a sea serpent, but ocular proof dispelled their conflicting doubts. Gracefully his serpentship coiled toward shore, and before turning away from the rocky coast, had ventured within two hundred yards of the campers. So far as could be judged, the marine monster was 100 feet or over in length and as large round as a barrel. The head was seen upright in the water, and when under the waves, the body floated on top of the waves . . . . Sumner D. York, heretofore a sceptic as to the sea serpent, is now a firm believer. He has seen it and no argument will change his belief.

In the coming years, tourists and locals alike would set a chair out by the shores of Gloucester Harbor, picnic, and watch for the sea serpent. One sailor, a ship's carpenter named Matthew Gaffney, not only saw the creature, but fired at him. Gaffney wrote:

> I had a good gun, and took good aim. I aimed at his head, and I think I must of hit him. He turned toward us immediately after I had fired, and I thought he was coming at us; but he sunk down and went directly under our boat, and made his appearance at about one hundred yards from where he sunk . . .

By the late 1800s, there had been so many reported sightings that the *Boston Globe* announced it would no longer cover the sightings as they had become routine. The fact the beast exists is no longer in question.

The most recent sighting of a sea serpent in Massachusetts occurred on July 25, 1962, off the coast of Marshfield. The Associated Press covered the story and told of witnesses on two separate fishing vessels (*The Vincy* and the *Carol Ann*) who saw the creature. The Marshfield serpent was described as having the head of an alligator and a body shaped like a nail keg. One of the fishermen, Archie Lewis, was quoted as saying that the creature was "gulping up the fish in the area and did not concern itself with fishermen in the way."

Since then, the sightings seemed to have stopped around Gloucester and Rockport. The predominant theory is that this giant serpent needed a lot of food, and perhaps the region was overfished and overcrowded with motorized boats, so the giant beast moved on to more hospitable waters.

Boston's Big Steaming Tea Kettle

BOSTON, MASSACHUSETTS

On New Year's Day of 1875, a crowd of thousands gathered in Boston in front of the Oriental Tea Company's Court Street storefront. Placed above the store was a giant golden tea kettle steaming from its spout. Its capacity: 227 gallons, 2 quarts, 1 pint, and 3 gills (a gill is 4 fluid ounces in very old measurements). The audacious wonder drew in customers from all over the city. By the 1960s, the neighborhood had declined considerably and was about to be razed to make way for Government Center. Though Oriental Tea Company didn't survive the transition, its kettle did, in a new location. The kettle became a fixture over Steaming Kettle Coffee Shop right outside of Government Center. The coffee shop changed hands over the coming decades until Starbucks took over the location in 1997, bringing the flavor of Seattle to Boston. At least they had the sense to keep the iconic kettle steaming.

Dogtown's Inspirational Boulders

GLOUCESTER, MASSACHUSETTS

The Bay State's most famous ghost town can be found in the woods of Cape Ann, straddling the town lines of Gloucester and Rockport. Originally settled in 1693, the hilltop village, then called the Commons Settlement, offered a little less bite from the winter winds on the coast, and the higher vantage point gave some protection against raiding pirates, however the land offered little else. The rocky soil made farming difficult, boulders were cast every which way, courtesy of the last Ice Age, which made building and getting around difficult. Still, the Commons was the place to be by 1730. Sixty of the most prominent families in Gloucester lived on Commons Road. The area was convenient in that it was central to Sandy Bay (the original name of Rockport), Pigeon Cove, Lanesville, and Annisquam.

After the War of 1812, the Commons was becoming a less desirable address. The only people left in town were widows and the poor—many of whom kept dogs as pets and for protection. Hence the name "Dogtown." Some estimate that there were over fifty Revolutionary War widows living in abject poverty in town. They lived on the abundant berries they could pick and preserve and anything else they could beg, borrow, or steal. People born in the Commons didn't return because industries like fishing were beginning to boom down by the water, and there was much better farmland elsewhere.

Some of the buildings left in Dogtown were rented out to the crews of fishing boats—a raucous bunch, to be sure—and Dogtown became the "Red Light District" of Gloucester. There were fortune tellers, witches, sex workers, and other characters who would be considered unsavory in other parts of town.

Around 1830, the residents finally gave up on the place for good, leaving the village to the dogs who once stood watch, but now were left to hunt and forage for themselves.

Fast-forward about a century when an eccentric named Roger Babson entered Dogtown history. As a child, Babson explored the many boulders and cellar holes there. In 1927, Babson wrote: "When on Dogtown Common, I revert to a boyhood which I once enjoyed when driving cows there many years ago . . . There is something inspiring in the huge barren hills and great boulders of Gloucester's Dogtown. At the same time, there are pathos and tragedy in the old forsaken cellars of the original inhabitants."

Roger Babson founded Babson College in Wellesley in 1919 and subscribed to a business philosophy that included the idea that when everyone works, the nation and business are stronger. During the Great Depression, it pained Babson to see so many people out of work. If there was no job to do, Babson would create one. He hired thirty-six unemployed quarry workers to carve mottoes into the many boulders left strewn around Dogtown. In Babson's 1935 autobiography, he wrote of his stone-carving endeavor: "Another thing I have been doing, which I hope will be carried on after my death, is the carving of mottoes on the boulders at Dogtown, Gloucester, Massachusetts. My family says that

NEVER TRY
NEVER WIN

SPIRITUAL
POWER

I am defacing the boulders and disgracing the family with these inscriptions, but the work gives me a lot of satisfaction, fresh air, exercise, and sunshine. I am really trying to write a simple book with words carved in stone instead of printed paper."

Today, as you hike through the trails of Dogtown, Babson's carved boulders grab your attention throughout the forest. Those that can still be seen include:

Save	Initiative
Ideas	Industry
Integrity	Truth
Loyalty	Be Clean
Never Try / Never Win	Get a Job
Prosperity Follows Service	Ideals
Keep Out of Debt	Be on Time
Use Your Head	Be True
Intelligence	Help Mother
Kindness	Spiritual Power
Courage	If Work Stops/Values Decay
Work	

Have a Nice Day . . . and Afterlife

WORCESTER, MASSACHUSETTS

The yellow smiley face is everywhere. You've likely received a text message in the last day or so with at least one smiley face emoji. In some phones and word processing applications, if you type a colon and a right-parenthesis next to it, you automatically get a smiley face: :) It's one of those things we assumed has existed in the collective consciousness of humans for millennia. If you search the hieroglyphs in the great pyramids in Egypt, you'd find one somewhere, right?

If you visit the grave of Harvey Ball (1921–2001) in Notre Dame Cemetery in Worcester, you'll see the smiley face staring back at you from both sides of his headstone. As you stare at the yellow icon on Ball's grave, if you find yourself sick of the omnipresent icon of happiness, and looking for the person to blame, just look down at your feet. Its creator lies below.

Harvey Ball was born and raised in Worcester. Interested in art from a young age, he found himself an apprenticeship with a local sign painter his junior year of high school. After graduation, he attended Worcester Art Museum School where he studied fine arts. However, his dreams of working as a commercial artist had to wait while Ball served in the army during World War II. Upon his return to Worcester, he began working with a local ad agency until he started his own firm in 1959.

BALL

In December of 1963, State Mutual Insurance company hired Ball to help them with a project. State Mutual had recently purchased another insurance company and employee morale was low as restructuring and reorganization took its toll. They asked Ball for a smiley face button. At first, he created a yellow circle with a smile, but realized that someone could turn that upside down, and then you have a frown. The solution? Add two eyes. Then it's always smiling. He could have used a compass and made all of the circles and lines perfect, but he felt that freehand gave it more character.

If you look closely, you'll see that the right eye is slightly larger than the left, and the smile on the right side of the grin is slightly thicker than the left. That's how you know you've got the real thing. The button project paid him $45 and took about ten minutes. It was never trademarked or anything like that because how big could something like that get? Right? RIGHT?!

A Mill Run by Satanic Imps

EASTON, MASSACHUSETTS

It's difficult to argue with an official sign—especially one erected and paid for by a town's taxpayers. (For one, the sign rarely argues back.) On Mill Street in Easton, one such historic sign is one you might pass daily and not bother to read. After all, it's a residential street, and there's a small cemetery a few hundred feet away on the opposite side. You're likely heading somewhere. But . . . if you read it, you may do a double take. The sign reads:

Mill Pond. Site of the sawmill built by John Selee in the 18th century and continued by his son, Nathan, a wizard who purportedly used satanic imps to run the mill at night. Easton Conservation Commission. 6.6 Acres. Acquired in 1999.

A wizard?! Satanic imps?!

By the mid-1700s, Easton was slowly growing, thanks in part to Bay Road, which cut through town. In order to speed up that growth, they needed a sawmill. Local resident John Selee saw a business opportunity, so he bought some land along the Poquanticut Stream, and built a mill. Waterpower drove the saw that cut trees into lumber. If the saw was in motion, Selee was making money. In time, the business prospered.

John brought his son, Nathan, to the mill often, telling his boy that this was the family business, and he should be ready to take it over some day. But Nathan wasn't all that interested in mill work. He was a dark, brooding young man who liked to wander off alone. Though Nathan would have rather pursued some other line of work, or better yet, just live off the profits of the mill, he eventually agreed to run the business. But soon rumors swirled that Nathan employed some unnatural help.

One evening, a local man was walking home late at night when he heard what he believed was the mill operating. But no mill can run in the dark! Once it was suggested that imps from hell were running the mill at night for dark and brooding Nathan Selee, the fates were sealed. The story of satanic imps operating the mill at night for their wizard master swirled for decades to come, even after the mill shut down in the late 1700s and had long rotted away.

Today what lies behind the sign is a wooded, swampy area, and just a few hundred feet away in the corner of the Selee Cemetery sits the grave of Nathan Selee who died August 24, 1815, at eighty-two years of age. If his ghost is still knocking about, he doesn't have a long commute to visit the site of his family's former mill.

ERECTED
in memory of
MR.
NATHAN SELEE.
who died
Aug. 24. 1815:
aged 82 years.

A Skeleton in Armor

FALL RIVER, MASSACHUSETTS

In May of 1831, Hannah Borden Cook was digging through a sandbank in what is now the intersection of Fifth and Hartwell Streets to collect sand to scour her floors for spring cleaning. While gathering sand, she unearthed a human skull.

The site was soon excavated to reveal the skeleton of a man wrapped in bark and bark cloth. The skeleton wore a triangular breastplate of brass and was adorned with a belt made of brass tubes. He was found in a sitting posture with the legs brought up nearly parallel with the body. He was armed with arrows tipped with brass arrowheads.

The archaeological find was put on display at the Fall River Athenaeum, where it sat for over a decade until a fire in 1843 destroyed downtown Fall River, including the Athenaeum.

The skeleton's existence was fuel for many wild theories as to its origin. In 1837, historian John Stark postulated that the skeleton was Egyptian or Phoenician.

Henry Wadsworth Longfellow was inspired by the find to pen the poem "The Skeleton in Armour" in 1841. The first stanza reads:

Speak! speak! thou fearful guest!
Who, with thy hollow breast
Still in rude armor drest,
Comest to daunt me!
Wrapt not in Eastern balms,
But with thy fleshless palms
Stretched, as if asking alms,
Why dost thou haunt me?

By 1881, historian Henry Chase noted that this burial was consistent with Wampanoag Indian burials of sachems, or great warriors.

Though lost to fire, Fall River never forgot about the unique find. In 1903, a plaque was erected to commemorate the place of Hannah Borden Cook's grisly discovery.

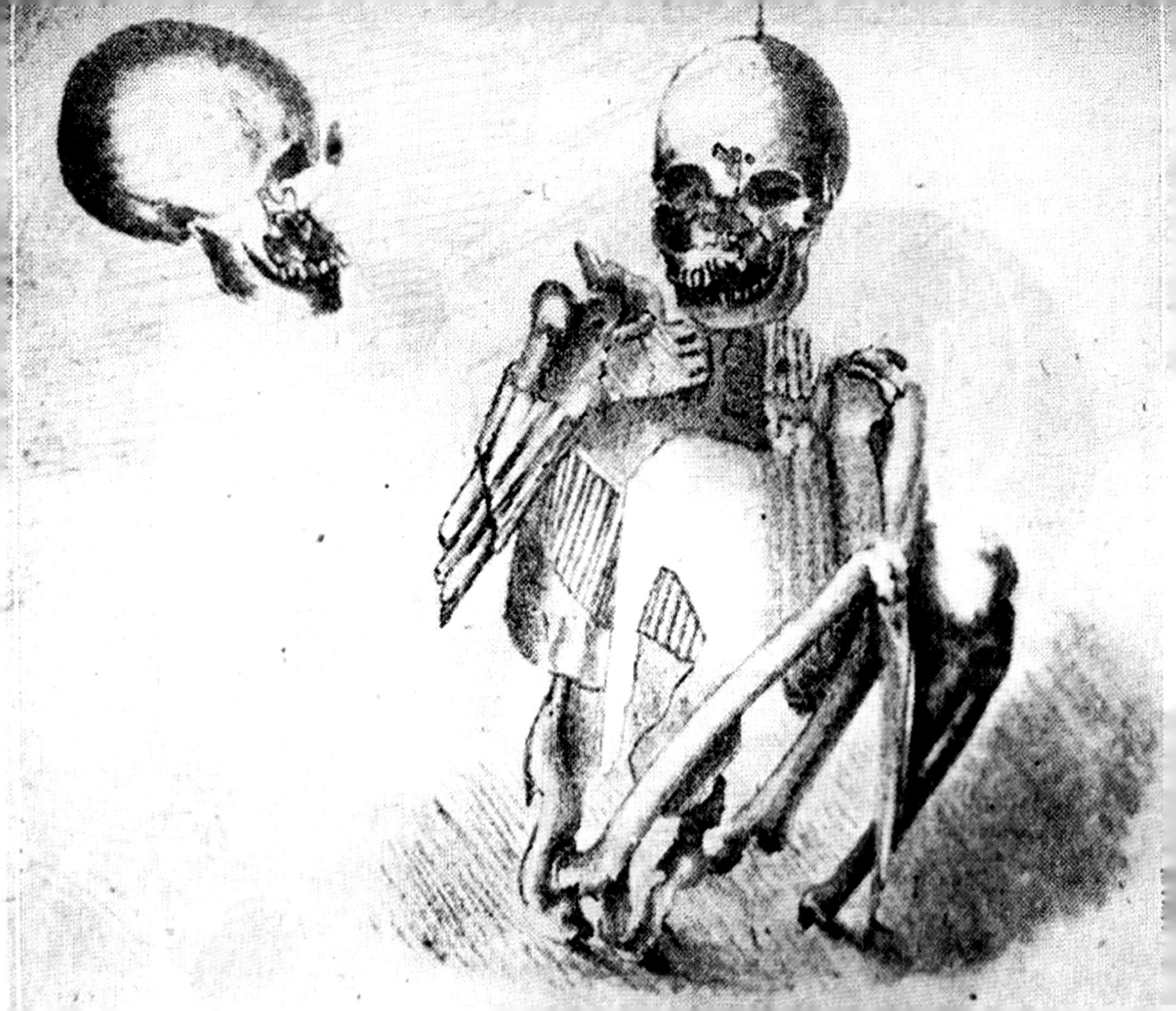

Ripton: Massachusetts's Most Mysterious Town

BERKSHIRE COUNTY, MASSACHUSETTS

The letterhead reads: TOWN OF RIPTON, MASSACHUSETTS, ESTABLISHED 1767.

The Commonwealth of Massachusetts has 292 towns and 59 cities, located in 14 counties. We can't fault you for not knowing all of them. Ripton, we're told, is located in Berkshire County in the western part of the state. A place where there is no Boston accent, in part out of protest because folks in this area of the state feel that the politicians in Boston don't pay any attention to them and hardly know they exist. If you ask Ripton town officials, they'll tell you there's truth to that, and they have the evidence to prove it.

In July of 1984, Ripton first made waves in Massachusetts for pulling off one of the greatest pranks in the history of the state. Locals were upset that hunters from the Boston area were making a mess of their environment. Plus, there was an extreme lack of stocked trout in the town's river and pond. So, after their annual town meeting—always held on June 31—they filed forms on town letterhead with legislators in Boston. They were seeking $50,000 for stocking trout and fixing up the shores of Lazy River in town, plus $10,000 for weed control and cleanup at Darey's Pond.

Those numbers seemed reasonable enough to the powers that be. The forms were submitted to the folks on Beacon Hill in Boston, and thankfully passed that year's annual budget for the state. Quoting directly from that year's state budget, it says, "A sum not exceeding fifty thousand dollars shall be used for riprap ['riprap' means to fortify the banks of the river with stones] and general stream maintenance of the Lazy River in Ripton . . . an amount not exceeding ten thousand dollars shall be used for weed control and cleanup at Darey's Pond in the town of Ripton." Governor Michael Dukakis signed off on the entire budget.

There you go. The town got what it asked for.

In the spring of 1985, the United States Air Force was looking for a location to construct some early-warning communication towers in Berkshire County. The town of Hawley, Massachusetts (located about fifteen miles west of Greenfield), looked like the perfect location for these towers. The only problem was the people of Hawley didn't want it. They felt the towers would mess up their beautiful skyline. The project was not welcomed by the locals, so they raised a fuss. That's when the first selectmen of Ripton stepped in and offered their town for the towers. They explained how their topography and location was pretty similar to the town of Hawley, so the Air Force sent some scouts to check it out.

The Air Force personnel drove through Berkshire County looking for Ripton, but there was only one problem: They couldn't seem to find it.

Before you go thinking the US Air Force is incompetent, it turns out there was a good reason they couldn't find Ripton. It doesn't exist. It never existed. The whole thing was a prank set up to prove that politicians in Boston pay no attention to the western part of the state.

So what happened to the $60,000 allocated for Ripton? It never arrived because the Massachusetts Department of Revenue couldn't find Ripton either. So the money sat in an escrow account until the jig was up, and it went back into the state treasury. The whole thing was a prank; the brainchild of George Darey (remember Darey Pond from the funds allocation?), the town selectman in Lenox, Massachusetts, and the chair of the state's Fisheries and Wildlife Board. He teamed up with some conservationist friends, including Berkshire Natural Resources Council cofounder George Wislocki and Lenox Land Trust cofounder Sally Bell. It was Bell who came up with the name Ripton.

Looking back, there were signs obviously missed by state officials. There is no body of water called Darey Pond or Lazy River in Massachusetts. You'd think after this prank was found out that they would have closed the loop on fake towns submitting requests for budget funds, but not so. In 1991, Ripton struck again when a proposal was launched to place a landfill along the Appalachian Trail in Hinsdale, Massachusetts. When the people of Hinsdale raised a stink, a letter arrived from Ripton town officials offering to host the landfill. Then, in 1992, Ripton made one last wave on Beacon Hill when the Ripton "Town Officials" asked for $400,000 to establish five positions to investigate the "predacious activities of the endangered Howame analyst." We're guessing "Howame" meant "House Ways and Means." The request made it to the preliminary budget, but then they were found out.

You'd think politicians would learn, but they never do. And that's part of the point of the prank. All of these small towns in Western Massachusetts—shoot, even central Massachusetts—often feel forgotten by lawmakers. Things have improved, but the bitterness is still there. You can't blame them for pulling a prank on occasion because sometimes a good prank forces changes. If politicians can't get it done, sometimes you gotta send in the clowns.

Most recently, two guys working on a book called *Wicked Strange* faked a photo of the town sign for their book. So the legend continues.

PAUL REVERE
LEXINGTON AND CONCORD.
THE OLD NORTH CHURCH
GIFT SHOP
REVOLUTION'S EDGE

One If by Land, Two If by Sea . . . Three If by Air?

BOSTON, MASSACHUSETTS

The Old North Church is one of Boston's most famous landmarks. As children we've all heard the tale of the Midnight Ride of Paul Revere, who looked up at this very steeple for lanterns to let folks know when and how the British were coming. "One if by land, two if by sea . . . " so the poem goes.

But the Old North Church has another story to tell . . . this one much less well-known, but arguably more profound. Just across from the church on a courtyard wall resides a plaque—you'd miss it if you didn't know what to look for—but it reads:

So wait . . . FLY?! Don't bother running to Google, we'll tell you right here that the Wright Brothers' first flight was December 17, 1903, in Kitty Hawk, North Carolina. Okay, okay, maybe the plaque is talking about balloon flight? Nope, the first manned balloon flight happened on October 19, 1783 in Paris, France, with Jean-François Pilâtre de Rozier, Jean-Baptiste Réveillon, and Giroud de Villette on board.

So what the hell happened here on September 13, 1757, and why isn't Boston internationally known as the first in flight?

It gets even worse! Not only did this event really happen, but that crazy SOB John Childs fired a pistol on his descent! Here's a quote from the September 23, 1757, *New Hampshire Gazette*: "Tuesday in the afternoon John Childs, who had given public notice of his intention to fly from the steeple of Dr. Cutler's Church, performed it to the satisfaction of a great number of spectators; and Wednesday in the afternoon he again performed it twice; the last time he set off with two pistols loaded, one of which discharged in his descent, the other missing fire, he cocked and snapped again before he reached the place prepared to receive him."

Digging a little deeper, we learn that Childs was a rope flyer—a kind of medieval daredevil who would tie a rope to a tall building, then secure it at an angle on the ground. Next, he would strap a plank of wood to his chest with a groove carved in it, then balance on the rope and zoom to the ground. The *New Hampshire Gazette* article continues:

"It is supposed from the steeple to the place where the rope was fixed was about 700 feet upon a slope, and that he was about 16 & 18 seconds performing it each time. As these performances led many people from their business, he is forbid[den] flying any more in the town. The said Childs says he has flown from the highest steeples in England, and off the Monument, by the Duke of Cumberland's Desire."

So John Childs flew from the steeple—multiple times—and then the city of Boston banned the practice making it against the law. So this jerk ruined it for all of us, but still, he gets a plaque.

Timothy Dexter: An Idiot Who Failed Upward

NEWBURYPORT, MASSACHUSETTS

In 1802, an idiot and eccentric from Newburyport published a memoir called *A Pickle for the Knowing Ones*. Timothy Dexter referred to himself as the "Greatest Philosopher in the Western World." His book has 8,847 words in it and is over 32 pages. There were 33,864 letters in the book, it was full of spelling and grammatical errors, and there's not a single bit of punctuation to be found on any page. In the book he complains about his wife, politicians, clergy, and anything else that came into his mind.

Here's a short excerpt from his book (good luck, editors!): "To mankind at Large the time is Com at Last the grat day of Regoising what is that why I will tell you thous three kings is Rased Rased you meane should know Rased on the first Royal Arch in the world"

What should have been a commercial flop went on to eight editions and printings. In the fourth edition, he answered his critics' complaining about no punctuation by adding an appendix with a page full of punctuation marks: commas, periods,

exclamation points, and so on. He told the reader to "peper (sic) and solt (sic) as they please."

Have you ever had the misfortune of working with someone so incompetent that they continue to get promotions and raises if for no other reason than to keep them away from the actual work that needs to be done because they would only make a mess of it? Those folks seem to fail upward until eventually they're running dysfunctional companies. That is the story of Timothy Dexter.

Dexter was never the sharpest knife in the drawer. He dropped out of school at age eight to work on a farm. Later he worked as a tanner's apprentice, and while he wasn't too bright, he did figure out there is one easy way for him to get wealthy: Marry a rich woman.

In 1769, twenty-two-year-old Dexter moved from Malden, Massachusetts, to Newburyport, where he set his sights on a wealthy widow named Elizabeth Frothingham who was ten years his senior. The wooing worked, the two were married, and Dexter purchased them a stately mansion with her money.

Dexter was comfortable for a little while, and content to sit in the lap of luxury as the American Revolution played itself out. By 1783 with the war over, Dexter was ready to make bigger financial moves. Colonists had been using Continental dollars, which were backed by the Royal Crown in England. But after the war was over, those banknotes were worthless. The new nation needed a new currency. Dexter purchased as many of the Continental dollars as he could. He was paying pennies on the dollar. This dolt didn't realize that these notes were no longer worth the paper they were printed on. Folks were happy to unload them for anything. The new United States government soon offered to buy these notes back at 1 percent of their value . . . but not Massachusetts. Massachusetts offered to buy those notes back on par, or equal value. Suddenly . . . this idiot just got a lot richer.

Here was this uneducated buffoon at the wealthy social parties in Newburyport. The local aristocracy couldn't stand him, so they tricked him. They convinced Dexter that he should buy as many bed warmers as he could afford—you know, those metal pans at the end of a long handle, which you fill with hot coals from the fire and use to warm your cold bed in the winter—and ship those bed warmers to the West Indies where he could sell them for a fortune.

The West Indies are, of course, in the Caribbean—tropical, and warm year-round. Still, Dexter acted on this faux tip and shipped a vessel full of bed warmers to the tropical islands. It should have been a total financial loss for this numbskull. But when the ship arrived, locals saw these bed warmers as perfect ladles for the molasses industry. The supply sold out and the ship sailed back to Newburyport flush with money.

The Newburyport aristocracy were baffled, but determined to ruin Dexter. So now they told him he simply must ship coal to Newcastle because there was a fortune to be made there in coal. What they knew and Dexter did not, was that Newcastle was one of the biggest coal producers in all of England. Dexter did no homework, he had his ship loaded with coal, and they sailed to Newcastle.

By the time Dexter's vessel arrived in Newcastle, the captain discovered there was a massive strike by coal miners. The output of coal had dropped to zero, so the captain was able to offload his coal into the cargo holds of waiting vessels at a huge premium. Once again, Dexter's ship sailed home full of money.

No matter what dumb move Dexter made, it turned into gold. In 1798, Dexter purchased a Newburyport palace. He had wooden statues of great men sculpted all over the property. There was George Washington, Thomas Jefferson, Napoleon, and, of course, Timothy Dexter.

At one point he faked his own death so he could spy on his own wake. Thousands attended and Dexter was furious that his wife didn't cry enough. Dexter left us his memoir in 1802 and died in 1806 (for real this time) at age fifty-nine. He was wealthy, famous, eccentric, and maybe not as dumb as we all thought.

New England's First Documented UFO

BOSTON, MASSACHUSETTS

The first UFO encounter over New England was documented by Governor John Winthrop. Winthrop was an English Puritan and one of the founders of the Massachusetts Bay Colony. He first took office in 1629 and would serve eighteen annual terms (though not consecutively) until his death in 1649.

On March 1, 1639, Winthrop noted the following in his published journal:

> In this year one James Everell, a sober, discreet man, and two others, saw a great light in the night at Muddy River. When it stood still, it flamed up, and was about three yards square; when it ran, it was contracted into the figure of a swine: it ran as swift as an arrow towards Charlton, and so up and down about two or three hours. They were come down in their lighter about a mile, and when it was over, they found themselves carried quite back against the tide to the place they came from. Divers[e] other credible persons saw the light, after, about the same place.

That's it. But, then again, there's nothing more to say. Yet, all the elements of a modern-day close encounter are there in that single paragraph. The witness is credible, according to Winthrop's sources, there were multiple witnesses, and there's even the element of missing time. "They were come down in their lighter [a small boat] about a mile, and when it was over, they found themselves carried quite back against the tide to the place they came from." So they watched this craft for some time and then found themselves back where they began their journey, which would seem to be impossible. As for the craft being the shape of a swine (or pig), Everell was a farmer, and that was a shape familiar to him.

We could all take a lesson from Governor Winthrop. There's no speculation as to the source, whether God, the Devil, or little green men. It was a weird enough event to document for the ages, and here we are documenting it again. You're welcome, Governor Winthrop.

Edith Wharton's Haunted Mount

LENOX, MASSACHUSETTS

No, I don't believe in ghosts, but I'm afraid of them.
—Edith Wharton

Pulitzer Prize winner Edith Wharton may (or may not) have believed in ghosts based on her famous quote, but those who visit her Lenox home, The Mount, have seen and experienced specters that make them wonder if maybe there's more to this mortal coil than meets the eye.

Edith Newbold Jones was born in 1862 to a wealthy New York City family. She spent her early years traveling Europe and learning French, German, and Italian. When she turned ten, her family returned to the United States.

By age fifteen, she'd finished her translation of a German poem titled "What the Stones Tell," though her family didn't want her name to appear in print because the names of upper-class women should only appear in birth, marriage, and death announcements. That chip, placed squarely on young Edith's shoulder at age fifteen, would help form one of the greatest literary artists in American history.

Edith married Edward "Teddy" Robbins Wharton in 1885, and though the two shared a love of travel and similar social standing, his acute depression made their marriage and her life hell. By 1902, the couple built The Mount in Lenox and resided there almost exclusively while Teddy wrestled with his demons. The lavish mansion was a prison for Wharton and her writing was her escape.

Inside The Mount, Wharton penned such classics as *Ethan Frome* and *The Age of Innocence*, but later in life she tackled her own fears and beliefs in the supernatural with *Tales of Men and Ghosts* and her collection *The Ghost Stories of Edith Wharton*.

Each night before bed, Edith Wharton would always place her slippers at the edge of her bed with the toes pointed toward the door. When asked why, she answered, "So the hobgoblins won't get me while I sleep."

In The Mount's library, staff have witnessed two people sitting in chairs by the fireplace reading books. They make no sound, and then fade from sight. It was in these very chairs that Wharton and her dear friend Henry James spent many hours poring through their favorite tomes.

From her work, her letters, and the stories of those who knew her at The Mount, there's no question that Wharton believed something was haunting her. And from the testimony of those who now work there, it still is.

New Hampshire

Born: June 21, 1788

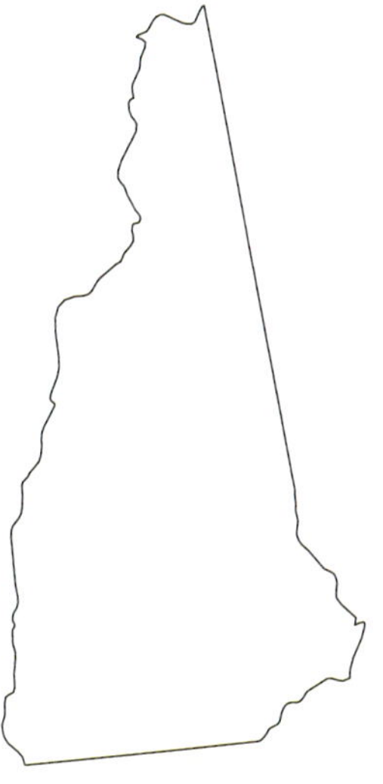

Home to New England's . . . *nay* . . . the *nation's* number-one most badass license plate motto of "Live Free or Die," New Hampshire is a place as tough as its famous granite, and as wild as the White Mountains that dot its interior.

A state of low taxes and cheap booze, it's only fitting that the motto's origins trace back to a toast made by New Hampshire's most revered Revolutionary War hero, General John Stark. Back on July 31, 1809, Stark's health was so poor that he was unable to attend a reunion of the Battle of Bennington, so he sent his regards by letter. The full toast was: "Live free or die: Death is not the worst of evils." However, historians back in 1809 knew the entire phrase would never fit on a license plate without making wider automobiles, so it was trimmed (which would prove fortunate close to a century later when the automobile was invented).

Though the famed "Old Man of the Mountain," which graced the face of Cannon Mountain for centuries, fell in 2003, New Hampshire has stuck with his profile on their state seal, route signs, and anything else where he'll fit.

Not saying Granite Staters are stubborn, but they can certainly hold a grudge, they are known for their eccentricities, they can dig in when they need to, and they know a thing or two about ghosts and UFOs, as well as Old Scratch who makes his presence and influence known throughout the state.

A Tombstone Tirade

MILFORD, NEW HAMPSHIRE

A headstone's epitaph *should* be a testament to a life. A birth date or birth year, a dash, and a death date or death year. Maybe a few words about what the person beneath your feet did with that dash. Accomplishments like: loving parent or spouse, perhaps some poetic quote that was meaningful to the deceased.

Then there's the marker of Caroline Cutter, who died in Milford, New Hampshire, in 1842. What flows on her headstone is 146 words of fury composed by her husband, and aimed at specific members of the church community in town.

Her epitaph reads:

> Caroline H., Wife of Calvin Cutter, M.D. Murdered by the Baptist Ministry and Baptist Churches As follows: September 28, 1838; aged 33. She was accused of lying in church meeting by the Rev. D. D. Pratt and Deacon Albert Adams. Was condemned by the church unheard. She was reduced to poverty by Deacon William Wallace When an ex parte council was asked of the Milford Baptist Church, by the advice of their committee, George Raymond, Calvin Averill, and Andrew Hutchinson. They voted not to receive any communication on the subject. The Rev. Mark Carpenter said he thought as the good old Deacon said, "We've got Cutter down and it's best to keep him down." The intentional and malicious destruction of her character And happiness as above described destroyed her life. Her last words upon the subject were "Tell the Truth and The Iniquity will come out."

An "ex parte council" (we had to look this up, too) is like an emergency meeting where a ruling body—usually a court of law—makes a quick decision without having all of the facts. Those legal decisions are supposed to be temporary until such time as a proper hearing can take place. But that didn't happen here.

The Baptist community of Milford had been growing to the point where they were going to need more space. For months, Dr. Calvin Cutter had been trying to get members of the congregation to fund the construction of a new church building. Dr. Cutter told other members of the congregation that he would put up much of his own money to fund this new church, but he needed some help.

While everyone loved the sound of a new church building, the logistics, finances, and everything else surrounding the project didn't seem realistic to many. Including the Rev. D. D. Pratt and Deacon Albert Adams. They suspected that Dr. Cutter was pulling some kind of scam. That maybe he wasn't willing to put up his own money after all, and maybe he was trying to swindle other members of the church into handing over their money to him. *That maybe he's skimming.*

At first, the reverend and the deacon tried to talk to Dr. Cutter. They reasoned that they should lead these fundraising efforts. But Dr. Cutter didn't give up. And his wife, Caroline, was

right there behind him. She did all she could to rally support in the church among the wives, who would hopefully influence their husbands.

The Cutters' efforts divided the church. Some perceived their actions as some kind of power play to try to gain more influence in the new church. Others suspected that Dr. Cutter was some kind of shyster.

In September of 1838, the Reverend Pratt and Deacon Adams had had enough. They accused Caroline Cutter of lying in a church meeting. The scandal rocked the church community, and pretty soon the church committee decided to kick the Cutters out of the church without giving them a chance to defend themselves. Once shunned by their church, Caroline became despondent. She was a broken shell of a person. Over the next few years, she deteriorated and passed away in 1842.

These kinds of things happen all the time in church communities. There's a disagreement on direction, internal power struggles, and sometimes people leave the church, others get kicked out. But Dr. Cutter never forgave their Baptist foes, and he let it be known on his wife's headstone. An editorial tirade that would last throughout the ages.

We can only hope the person who carved the stone was paid by the word.

A Redstone Missile on the Town Green

WARREN, NEW HAMPSHIRE

File this under: You don't see *that* every day. When driving down Water Street through the center of Warren, you'll see things you'd expect to see in any small New England town. There's the white-steepled church, the town hall, a town gazebo, the town green, and a seventy-three-foot-tall Redstone short-range ballistic missile.

The Redstone missile could carry a warhead about 175 miles and was in service mainly in Europe during the cold war between 1958 and 1964. A modified version of this missile was used to launch New Hampshire native Alan Shepard into suborbital flight, making him the second person, and the first American, to travel into space.

In the early 1970s, a Warren man named Ted Asselin was stationed with the US Army at Redstone Arsenal in Alabama. He saw these surplus missiles lying in a grassy field, so he asked if he could take one home to Warren and put it on display (as one does).

The Army agreed, as long as the missile was gutted of its engine and guidance systems. Which is too bad: Imagine the weight you could throw around with other towns in the region when negotiating things like water rights, highway redirections, and landfill locations. "Well sure, we *could* pay a price increase or . . . " (then you gesture toward the missile on the town common and end the negotiations).

USA
USA
SPEED
LIMIT
10
USA

So the army told Asselin that as long as it didn't cost them any money to deal with it, Warren could have the missile. Asselin agreed, the town of Warren agreed, and mostly at his own expense, Asselin got the missile up here in 1971, where it's been on display ever since.

The Haunted Mt. Washington Hotel

BRETTON WOODS, NEW HAMPSHIRE

Sitting in the shadow of New England's highest peak—and the building's namesake—the Mt. Washington Hotel hearkens back to the days in the early 20th century when big hotel resorts were playgrounds for those who could afford the getaway.

In 1900, Joseph Stickney plunked down $1.7 million of his own money to construct this giant hotel. Stickney hired 250 Italian artisans for the construction. Following a European superstition, they varied the number of steps to the second floor in order to confuse the ghosts. There are thirty-three steps up from the registration area, and thirty-one steps up from the South Tower.

"Look at me, gentlemen," Stickney said in his opening speech on July 28, 1902, "for I am the poor fool who built all of this." He wouldn't live long enough to enjoy his new building. Stickney died suddenly a little over a year after the hotel opened.

After Stickney passed away, his young widow, Carolyn, inherited the hotel. She became known as the Princess after she married French royalty, Prince Jean Baptiste Aymon de Faucigny-Lucinge. Princess Carolyn spent many summers here throwing lavish parties, always making sure she was the best-dressed woman in the room.

It's said that Carolyn would peek over the balcony at the guests below before she dressed for the evening so she could be sure to outshine all of the others. After Carolyn's death in 1936, caretakers reported seeing the lights go on and the Princess descending the staircases during the closed winter months.

Today, some people report catching a glimpse of a woman by the balcony looking around below before she disappears. If you don't spot her ghost, the hotel had the good sense to hang a giant painting of her near the registration desk, complete with a faux banister in front of the painting.

If there's one particular paranormal hot spot in the hotel, it's Room 314, better known as the Princess Room. Her four-poster bed still resides in the suite. Guests have reported waking up to see a woman sitting at the edge of the bed brushing her hair.

Hotels are transient places. It can be difficult to put a name on everything that bumps in the night, but some previous guests stick out. Carolyn *was* the princess of this castle in the White Mountains. This was the place where she was always the belle of the ball. We shouldn't blame her for never leaving.

It would seem that altering the number of steps to and from the second floor did little to discourage the ghost of Princess Carolyn.

English Jack—The Hermit of the White Mountains

CRAWFORD NOTCH, NEW HAMPSHIRE

A hermit, by definition, is a person who walks away from society to live on their own. We're intrigued by them because we wonder if they've found some divine answer to the meaning of life. Though their only wish is to be left alone, we sometimes seek them out anyway. English Jack, the hermit of the White Mountains, understood this well and used it to his advantage.

Back in the late 1800s, the White Mountains of New Hampshire were quickly becoming a tourist destination. Trails, roads, and even rails could take visitors to see the majestic beauty of New England's tallest mountains. The Portland and Ogdensburg Railroad, which started operating through Crawford Notch back in 1867, could bring you right to the heart of the White Mountains. The influx fueled local economies, and the savvy cashed in.

As soon as you stepped off the train at Crawford Notch, a hand-painted sign read: COME MEET ENGLISH JACK—THE HERMIT OF THE WHITE MOUNTAINS, with an arrow pointing the way.

Another sign or two along the trail led you to a ramshackle building that English Jack referred to as his ship. English Jack was a white-haired old man, originally from England. He spent the warmer tourist season in a shack on the mountain. Inside was basically a gift shop. English Jack sold trinkets, homemade beer, postcards, and his autobiography, written in rhyming verse. The enterprising "hermit" knew his story would draw in enough people to earn himself a living. Ask a few questions of Jack, and he'd suggest you buy his book. His 1891 autobiography begins:

> Good morning, Captain, you are here, I see.
> Well, take a seat till I think just a bit.
> I was foolish yesterday to agree
> To tell my yarn—I seldom speak of it —
> For forty years I've tried hard to forget,
> But some things burn into a fellow's brain.
> And even now, in moments of regret,
> I seem to live my whole life over again.

According to his book, John Alfred "Jack" Vials was born in London, England, in 1824. He was orphaned at age twelve and, with nowhere else to go, he took to the streets to find any job he could. After stumbling across a young girl named Mary Simmonds, who was crying because she'd lost her father in the crowd by the docks, Jack sprang into action and was able to locate her dad, Bill, and reunite him with his daughter. Bill Simmonds heard the boy's tale and invited him to stay at their home.

Soon Jack became a cabin boy for Captain Bill Simmonds. For eight years they sailed the seas together; all the while Jack was becoming an able seaman. In 1844, the ship they were sailing was wrecked in a storm on the Indian Ocean with most of the forty-two on board perishing. But thirteen survivors, including Jack and Bill, managed to make it to a remote island where they lived for nineteen months, waiting for rescue. In that time, thirteen survivors dwindled to four, with Jack and Bill among the remaining. But when Simmonds turned ill, he made Jack promise to find

a way home to care for his wife and daughter. Jack agreed. Soon, he was the only survivor left.

Jack was eventually rescued and made his way back to London, where he learned that Bill's wife had died, and his orphaned daughter had been forced to live in a workhouse. Jack immediately bought Mary's way out of the workhouse, placed her in a private school, and promised to return to marry her once he earned enough money back out at sea.

A year later, Jack returned to take his bride to their new life together, but soon learned that Mary had died from illness over the winter. No longer caring whether he lived or died, Jack joined the Royal Navy, figuring he'd die for his country.

Jack's poem tells of fighting in many battles, of fighting in Africa to free the slaves, to the arctic circle in search of Sir John Franklin's crew, and surviving the Crimean War. After years at sea, so much bloodshed, and no chance to offer his own life for God or country, Jack made his way to America where he found work building the railroad in New Hampshire. He liked the area so much, he decided to build himself a shack . . . or ship, as he called it, in the mountains around Crawford Notch, and live out the rest of his days telling his story to anyone who would listen.

The final lines of his book read:

I left old England then for good and all,
And do not think I ever shall go back;
I've waited long for death to sound my call,
But still I'm here. Your humble servant, Jack.

In his later years, Jack spent the summers in his shack, and the winters with families in towns below the mountain. He always dressed formally for dinners and was in every way the perfect houseguest, but once spring rolled around, he'd put on battered clothes and head back up into the mountain to be English Jack once more.

Jack died April 24, 1912, while staying with the McGee family. He was eighty-seven years old.

Chicken Farmer I Still Love You

NEWBURY, NEW HAMPSHIRE

We're all the romantic sort to some degree. We recognize grand gestures of love, even if they aren't directed at us. Even if they're confusing. We mean *really* confusing . . . and weird. It doesn't matter. Someone professed their love for another and that gives us all a little hope in a world that desperately needs more hope and love. When driving on Route 103 in Newbury, you may notice one such grand gesture painted on a boulder beside the road. It reads: Chicken Farmer I Still Love You.

Originally painted over fifty years ago, the paint has been maintained long after the love that inspired the words had faded.

Back in the spring of 1973, the Rule family lived across the street from this now-famous landmark rock. The house wasn't that large, but the yard had plenty of space for a vegetable garden and a few chickens.

CHICKEN
FARMER
I STill LOVE
YOU

Among those living inside was high school senior named Gretchen Rule. Like many high school seniors, she had her whole life ahead of her. There was a prom coming up, college, jobs, and endless adventures. One morning Gretchen was leaving her house when she saw that a message had been painted on the boulder across the street. It read: CHICKEN FARMER I LOVE YOU.

At first, Gretchen didn't know what to make of it, but soon figured out that someone had a crush on her and chose to express it with graffiti. Each day she read the message as she left her driveway. It was odd. But also kinda sweet.

Though the love was unrequited, the gesture was kind enough. Gretchen graduated from high school, and life moved on for everyone in Newbury. Months melted into years, then to decades. The message on the rock faded until you could hardly read it anymore ... Until ...

... Until the early 1990s when someone painted over the old graffiti and added one new word: CHICKEN FARMER I STILL LOVE YOU.

The message was back! No doubt marking nostalgia for those in town who remembered, but also annoying some uppity newcomers who in 1997 complained to the state of New Hampshire about the graffiti until the state came and painted over it with a reddish-colored square on the face of the rock.

For the first time in twenty-four years, there was no message. That's when the people of Newbury stepped up and said: *Wait a minute!* Nobody *paints over graffiti in our town without our okay!* The message was down only a few days before someone repainted the boulder: CHICKEN FARMER I STILL LOVE YOU.

But repainting wasn't enough. So, the people of Newbury signed a petition that said the chicken farmer sign should be left alone forever. The petition was submitted to the state of New Hampshire, and the state agreed to leave it alone.

Still, paint fades—especially in New Hampshire winters. And underbrush grows. Yet someone maintains this rock. When underbrush and trees continued to grow around it, someone would cut them back. When the paint faded, someone would come repaint. After more than fifty years, it's safe to say that this rock is now a town landmark. But the question remains: Who painted the original?

This rock of ages seems to make the news every few years. *Yankee Magazine* once did a feature story on it. Newspapers have covered it. New Hampshire Public Radio did a great story on it back in 2017. Gretchen Rule Hamel has commented in these various articles and stories that she has an idea of who her admirer was, but didn't want to say publicly. The New Hampshire Public Radio piece even went on to say that they were able to track down someone who said they knew for sure, but they kept the name private.

So the original author will remain a mystery. And that's part of the charm. If we knew the whole story and everything about it, the truth would never match our sweet imaginations. Because it's vague, we get to think of all the backstories there could be behind a simple message of love ... on the rocks.

The Great Wall of Sandwich

SANDWICH, NEW HAMPSHIRE

There are myriad reasons a person embarks on a grand construction project. Some want to leave their mark, to become immortal. Others see an opportunity for artistic expression on a great scale. Sometimes construction happens out of necessity—like building a bridge. But when a big construction project is undertaken out of spite, you know there's a good story there. That's the case with the Great Wall of Sandwich.

This Great Wall is five or six feet tall—depending on where you're standing—ten feet wide, and clearly square and well-built. It runs about a thousand feet down Little Pond Road, before turning northwest into the woods. The whole wall sits on private property, but there's plenty you can see from the street. How it got here is a story that dates back more than two centuries.

In the summer of 1824, twenty-two-year-old Isaac Adams was rubbing folks in town the wrong way. When he turned twelve, Isaac spent three years working at a cotton mill in Dover, New Hampshire, before taking an apprenticeship with a cabinet maker, which is what eventually landed him in the town of Sandwich. He was ambitious. Focused. He had big dreams. This small town wasn't big enough for Isaac. He figured if he could just get to Boston, maybe he could make his fortune. The only problem was this: Isaac was broke.

Adams reached out to his wealthy boss for a loan, but his boss brushed him aside. In a fury, the young man proclaimed to his boss that he was going to scrimp and save his way to Boston, and one day he would return to Sandwich and buy not only his boss's farm, but every farm in town!

True to his word, Adams saved every penny to get himself to Boston where he found work as a machinist working on printing presses. He couldn't help but see the flaws in the machines and ways they could be improved. He soon designed and developed a steam-powered press that revolutionized the industry. It sped up production significantly. Faster production meant lower costs for books, making the printed word that he loved so much available

KEEP OUT

to more people. By 1828, the twenty-six-year-old Isaac Adams was on his way to fortune.

In the coming decades, hundreds of print shops around the world acquired an Adams Steam Press, all the while making its inventor wealthy. He bought real estate in Boston, but never stopped thinking about the small town of Sandwich, New Hampshire.

In 1859, Adams sold his steam press patent for $100,000 and turned his manufacturing company over to his youngest son. Adams was determined to keep his word about buying up the farms back in Sandwich, where he planned to retire.

Adams, his wife Anna, and their three youngest children moved to Sandwich. First, he bought the old Clough House on the Sandwich Academy land. In the coming years he expanded the house, plus built other buildings on the property. Then he bought land. Lots of it. Eventually, he acquired 2,600 acres in Sandwich and the neighboring town of Moultonborough. Adams saw himself as a land baron. Lord of his castle. He hired groundskeepers, and paid top dollar to have statues and landscaping placed around his vast property.

Having acquired several statues in Europe, Adams wanted some of these works proudly displayed, and that's when he came up with an idea for a wall. A great wall that would encompass his entire property and feature these statues on top of the wall for all to see.

One hundred men and fifty yoke of oxen were employed to construct the wall. During the building project, Adams got involved in local politics. He was stubborn and vengeful, still carrying that grudge since he first left town. Adams wanted to run this town. He was elected selectman, representative to the General Court, moderator of the Town Meeting, and treasurer of the School Fund Note, which oversaw funds for the poor. He was as ambitious as ever, and didn't take kindly to criticism.

Adams wanted things his way, no matter what logic or anything else might dictate. He even looked into building a canal to connect Little Pond on his property to Lake Winnipesaukee. His idea was to make Little Pond a saltwater pond so he could raise lobsters and other saltwater fish. No matter how many people told him this would never work, the stubborn Adams never stopped thinking about his own supply of fresh lobsters. Though he didn't get his saltwater pond, he did get his Great Wall—a testament to his greatness adorned with statues for all to see. The statues are long gone, with the lone exception of Niobe from Greek mythology. She still stands on the Great Wall to spite any who ever doubted the young scrappy cabinetmaker all those years ago.

A Sermon from Beer Bottle Church

HAMPTON FALLS, NEW HAMPSHIRE

Dearly beloved, we are gathered here today to bow our heads to an ornament that sits atop the steeple of the First Baptist Church in Hampton Falls. Though folks in the congregation may insist it's simply called a "finial," anyone with even one working eye can look up and say: "Dude, that's a beer bottle!"

The origins of this church could be pulled straight from the Old Testament. The great earthquake of October 29, 1727, shook Hampton Falls. Houses quivered, some chimneys crumbled, and the ground split open. When the quake ended, the hill where this church now sits was covered in a bluish sand, and they say the air reeked of sulfur and brimstone, which is how it got the name Brimstone Hill.

In 1836, the town figured this was the perfect place to build a meetinghouse church. If the Devil tried once to come up through this crack in the Earth, their church would serve as the perfect cap on that diabolical bottle.

The First Baptist Church in Hampton Falls used the meetinghouse as their sanctuary, and the congregation grew. After a few decades, they needed more room. More donations poured in to the point where in 1859 they had the funds to expand the meetinghouse into a proper church. They even planned a tall, fancy white steeple.

That's when the Dodge Family offered to pony up $200 to fund a decorative topper for the steeple, and hired a fancy-pants Boston firm to make it. When it was completed and placed on top of the steeple, everyone stood back to admire the ornate work and the "finial" at the top.

Lest you think beer bottles back then looked radically different than they do today . . . they didn't. Shortly after the steeple was finished (we assume), some red-blooded, beer-drinking, Live-Free-or-Die Granite Stater walked by the congregation and said, "Dude, that's a beer bottle!" So, minutes after construction was completed, the Beer Bottle Church nickname was born and will remain until they either take it down, or the modern-day beer bottle undergoes a radical new design.

Amen.

Ruth Colbath: A Woman Who Waited

ALBANY, NEW HAMPSHIRE

Located just off the Kancamagus Highway near Conway, sits an old and unassuming farmhouse where one window was illuminated by a lantern each night for decades. The light was placed by Ruth Colbath to serve as a beacon in the night, in hopes that her husband, Thomas, might find his way home. Ruth waited a long time . . . but not quite long enough.

This simple one-and-a-half-story farmhouse was built in the early 1830s by Thomas Russell and his son, Amzi. They owned 8,700 acres of prime timberland, which is how they figured they'd make their fortune. Eventually, Amzi married a woman named Eliza, and they moved into this farmhouse, where they raised five daughters. In 1877, Amzi Russell died, leaving behind a mortgage and unpaid taxes on all of that land. Most of it was sold to pay his debts, but the farmhouse and its hundred-acre lot stayed in the family. Ten years later, Amzi's widow, Eliza Russell, deeded the property over to her daughter, Ruth Priscilla, and her husband Thomas Alden Colbath. But there was a catch . . . Thomas and Ruth got a free house, but mom/mother-in-law was going to live with them.

For a little while, Ruth and Thomas Colbath settled into their simple farm life. In 1890, Ruth became the first postmistress of the new Passaconaway Post Office, where she served as the hub of not just mail but all of the town gossip. Thomas tried his best to be a farmer, but he was growing restless.

In late September 1891, forty-one-year-old Thomas Colbath finished his daily chores, walked back to the house, grabbed a few items, and told his wife, Ruth, that he'd be back in a little while.

A few hours passed, and night fell. Ruth moved Thomas's dinner to the back of the stove to keep it warm, then placed a lantern in the window to help him find his way back. After more hours passed, Ruth grew concerned. By the time the sun came up the following morning, she was worried that something was horribly wrong.

Friends searched the road to Conway, but found no clues. They thought he might have been mauled by a bear or killed and robbed by highwaymen. The following night Ruth once again hung a lantern in the window for her husband. More days passed, and each night she placed the lantern. Yet, no word came from Thomas.

What we'd learn much later was that Thomas Colbath walked away from his old life. He made his way to Cuba, then over to Panama, where he joined a crew digging the Panama Canal. Then he moved to the western United States, where he worked on the railroad. All the while he kept moving, finding what work he could, then moving on again.

Months turned to years, yet each night Ruth Colbath hung that lantern in her window in hopes that her husband would return. In 1905, Eliza Russell passed away, leaving Ruth truly alone.

Everyone in the region knew of Ruth's story. Most knew by this point that Thomas was either dead, or he had started a new life somewhere else. Ruth's sister who lived in Portsmouth, New

Hampshire, begged her to come live with her, but she wouldn't leave her farmhouse and her life. Ruth could have had Thomas declared dead, she could have remarried, but she didn't. She kept lighting that lantern each night. All the while Thomas was globe-trotting wherever the wind took him.

By 1930, Ruth's health was failing. A family friend took Ruth from her home against her wishes to get her to a hospital, where she soon passed away. The lantern that had burned in her window for thirty-nine years would not be lit again.

In September of 1933, something extraordinary happened. An old man arrived in Carroll County, New Hampshire. He was a stranger, but somehow looked familiar. At eighty-three years of age, Thomas Colbath had finally come home. Since he'd left his wife and their little farmhouse forty-two years earlier, the airplane had been invented, electricity was harnessed and became widely available in homes, radio station broadcasts reached almost every house, and even the television had come along.

Thomas Colbath became a bit of a celebrity at that point. The area newspapers all printed interviews with him, in which he talked about his adventures. Old and frail, he had come home to die and held out hope that he might get the chance to do that in the farmhouse he once called home.

It's easy to feel sorry for Ruth and all of her wasted years waiting, but maybe she liked the solitude. Maybe not answering to anyone suited her just fine and if all she had to do was hang a lantern in the window to get that freedom, then it was a small price to pay. Or maybe Ruth's definition of "back in a little while" was simply radically different than her husband's.

It Gives Us the "Willeys"

CRAWFORD NOTCH, NEW HAMPSHIRE

Have you ever heard a story that gave you the willies? A tale so terrifying that a chill runs up your spine because, when you hear it, you know that whatever fate befell the person or people involved in the story could have happened to you?

Nestled in the White Mountains at Crawford Notch is a monument to a disaster that will give anyone a case of the willies.

Back in 1825, the White Mountains were just starting to attract tourists. Roads and rails were being built to get visitors closer, so there were opportunities to cater to those tourists. Samuel Willey Jr. of Bartlett, New Hampshire, his wife, Polly, their five children, and two hired men moved about ten miles northwest and purchased a small cabin called the Old Notch House. It was built in 1793 but had been purchased in 1823 by Ethan Crawford.

Crawford was an early White Mountain guide. He bought this house to serve as lodging for some of his guests who wanted to explore the mountains with him. Eventually, this area became known as Crawford Notch. After just a couple of years, Crawford decided he'd rather be in the mountain business than the innkeeping business, so he sold the house to Samuel Willey Jr.

Samuel Willey Jr. *did* want to be in the innkeeping business. When he arrived, he found the cabin in rough shape. The structure was dilapidated, there was a small clearing in front of the house, a trail that led down to the Saco River, and no neighbors around for miles. The Willey family and their hired hands spent a year expanding the cabin and turning it into an inn with rooms for guests, plus space for the Willey family.

Willey knew a road was under construction nearby that would give visitors easy access to his inn. In short, he was taking a big financial gamble that he hoped would soon pay off.

During that year, Willey observed his environment. He saw how the Saco River nearly dried up in the summer, and in the spring with the snowmelt, it could turn into raging rapids.

On June 26, 1826, a work crew of men were toiling away, clearing trees for the eventual turnpike. Suddenly, a heavy rainstorm hit. The rain came down in buckets, flash-flooding the valley and forcing the men to take shelter with the Willey family. As they watched the storm, Samuel Willey saw a great landslide start up on the mountain. Rock and debris poured down the side of the mountain, carving a scar right to the valley floor near the turnpike construction.

Polly Willey also saw the landslide and wanted to leave, to hitch up the horses and try to find shelter far away, but Samuel said they would be safer staying put and waiting out the storm.

When the storm subsided, the family was shaken, but everyone was safe.

Samuel Willey knew that landslide could have just as easily happened right behind his house. He needed to do something to protect his family, so he constructed a shelter for his family away from the house. He turned a horse cart on its side, and reinforced the structure with rocks so they could take shelter behind it should a landslide wash down the mountain behind them.

With the shelter built, and the rain now long gone, the Willeys settled back into the routine of their lives. They cared for

WILLEY BOULDERS
THIS OUTCROPPING OF ROCKS
SAVED THE WILLEY HOUSE FROM
DESTRUCTION ON AUG. 28.1826

livestock, they farmed, they took in the occasional traveler. But the summer of 1826 posed another problem . . . it was dry. One of the worst droughts the region had ever seen. The Saco River dried up. There was no rain in sight.

On Sunday, August 27, 1826, Samuel Willey's brother, Benjamin, was serving as a Congregational minister down in North Conway, New Hampshire, about twenty miles from Crawford Notch. He was driving his horse-drawn carriage back home when he noticed black, ominous clouds above. He later wrote, "The clouds reminded one of some heavy armed legions moving slowly and steadily into battle . . . covering mountains . . . fold after fold with their solemn dark drapery."

By midnight, the skies opened up. It was a deluge. In the White Mountains, so much water had drained from the soil that the dirt was loose. Trees and shrubs couldn't grip the ground as they normally would. The winds pushed the treetops in every direction as the water raced down the mountainside, picking up those loose shrubs and trees and creating flash floods and a massive landslide. The Saco River bed filled and then swelled in a matter of hours. Samuel Willey and his family knew they were in peril . . .

By Tuesday the storm had passed through. Local diaries noted how much damage there was in the valley from uprooted trees, floodwaters, and boulders that had been tossed like marbles. Meanwhile, a man named Kim Barker was traveling through Crawford Notch heading home. By late afternoon the Saco River high waters had dropped down enough to allow Barker to pass. Since it was getting dark, Barker made for the Willeys' inn for the evening.

When Barker pulled up, he was relieved to see the house was perfectly intact. The barn behind the house had suffered major damage from a landslide, and he noted two dead horses nearby. From inside the house, the Willeys' dog let out a mournful bark. Slowly, Barker approached the house and stepped inside to find the dog cowering. There was no damage to the house, though it looked like someone had left in a hurry. The beds were unmade, and the family Bible lay open on the kitchen table. Barker turned to go back outside and look for the Willeys, but found no sign of them. With fading light, he knew he'd need to wait for morning.

The next day, Barker sent word that the Willey family was missing. By Thursday, search parties came from all over the region to try to find them. As searchers combed through debris near the house, they made a gruesome discovery . . . the mangled bodies of Samuel and Polly Willey, along with the body of their youngest child, and the body of one of their hired hands, David Allen, had all been crushed within the mess of their makeshift horse cart shelter. A few days later, the body of the Willeys' eldest child, twelve-year-old Eliza Ann, was discovered drowned in the river. The body of the other hired hand, David Nickerson, was found as well. But the bodies of the other three children were never seen again.

The search party could clearly see how the landslide had hit a giant boulder on the hill behind the house, then split in two directions, sparing the house by going around it on both sides. Had the family remained in their home, they would have been unharmed. That fact combined with the monument that now sits near the boulder that spared the home is enough to give anyone . . . the willies.

The Immortal Doc Benton

MT. MOOSILAUKE, NEW HAMPSHIRE

Mt. Moosilauke in the White Mountains of New Hampshire is a buffet of high strangeness. At 4,802 feet, it's one of the famed forty-eight 4,000-footers in New Hampshire. The name *Moosilauke* is an Abenaki word that roughly translates to "bald place," referring to the rocky summit above the tree line.

Most of what we know of this legend is told by the students at Dartmouth College, which lies about forty miles to the southwest of Moosilauke.

Hiking the White Mountains can be dangerous. Not only do bears and other wild animals roam the mountains, but the weather conditions can change in minutes. If you hike the mountain approaching from the northeast at Kinsman Notch, you follow part of the Appalachian Trail. About halfway to the summit is Jobildunk Ravine, where they say three young men named William, Joseph, and Duncan went missing back in the winter of 1880.

The story goes that after three hours of hiking, the three boys noticed the skies darkening, but figured that even if it began to snow, they would be at most two hours from shelter. When the snow and wind began to whip, they did their best to follow their tracks back the way they came, but soon they found they needed to seek shelter under the canopy of a large pine tree. The three shivered together hoping it was just a squall, but, as the minutes turned to hours, it was clear they were in trouble.

That's when Joseph announced that if he didn't start moving, he was going to freeze. He was leaving the crude shelter to try to find help as fast as possible. After more hours passed, William and Duncan realized that when night fell and the temperature dropped, they would be doomed. Moving along was also their best hope.

The following day with the storm over, search parties looked for signs of the three boys, but no trace of them was found. When spring's melt came, they still found nothing. They say the ravine was named in memory of Joe, Bill, and Duncan: Jobildunk.

Some locals shrug at the mystery and figure that this was just one of those things that can happen in the White Mountains. But the students at Dartmouth will tell you the three young men were abducted by the immortal Doc Benton.

If we flash back to the spring of 1816, and travel thirty miles southwest of Mt. Moosilauke to the town of Hanover, New Hampshire, love was in the air.

Dr. Thomas Benton came from a prominent family. He studied medicine at a university in Germany. Though Benton was doing well in his studies, he didn't really fit in with the other students. He was a loner. Still, one older professor took a liking to him. Maybe because he was lonely, Benton ignored the rumors and whispers regarding some of the ungodly experiments this old professor had been conducting.

After the old professor died, Benton took some of his ancient books and an old, locked chest back to his home in New Hampshire. Back home, Benton fell in love with a local woman. Soon,

the two were engaged to be married, but a dark cloud gathered over the nuptials when the woman was struck by typhoid.

Whatever Dr. Benton learned in his regular classes or from this mysterious professor was not enough to save the life of his fiancée who succumbed to her illness. After her death, Doc Benton snapped. He took his old books, that old chest from his professor in Germany, and moved into the woods of Mt. Moosilauke, where he began to experiment with elixirs that could potentially grant eternal life.

Over the years, farm animals went missing. Sometimes loggers disappeared, and even hikers . . . after all, Doc Benton needed subjects for his experiments.

The students at Dartmouth will tell you that Doc Benton succeeded with his elixir. He even took his own medicine and is still out there today . . . but immortality came at a steep price, because now he's lost his mind. Hikers report seeing him run through the woods and then vanish, or they may hear his maniacal laugh in the wind that whips around the mountain. If the weather on Mt. Moosilauke doesn't get you, beware . . . Doc Benton might!

A Contract for Murder with the Devil

SOMERSWORTH, NEW HAMPSHIRE

"The Devil made me do it" is one of the oldest excuses for any crime, from the most minor misdemeanor to the most egregious felony. But in an old bank building in downtown Somersworth, there may be something to a contract with Old Scratch and a brutal murder that took place back in 1897.

The date was April 16, 1897. Good Friday. Folks in Somersworth were looking forward to the Easter weekend. At the Great Falls National Bank, business was pretty quiet. The bank had opened in 1845. Business was good enough that by 1874, a new building was constructed on the same site. The ground floor was home to a harness store, the second floor served as the bank, and the third floor was a meeting space for the Knights of Pythias.

On April 16, 1897, only two employees were on duty at the bank: Joseph Stickney, the sixty-eight-year-old bank cashier and treasurer, and his assistant, twenty-year-old Parchie Swasey. Stickney had been working for the bank for thirty-five years. He was a fixture in town, known by just about everyone.

When the noon bell rang, Stickney told his assistant she could go take her lunch hour. He was going to stay behind at the bank a short while longer before closing up the bank to take his lunch. It was ten past noon when Stickney heard the proprietor of the harness shop downstairs lock his doors for his lunch break. That's when a somewhat dashing young man in his mid-twenties entered the building. He was sporting a goatee and mustache, and was wearing a derby hat. To Stickney, the customer looked vaguely familiar. A man looking about the same had been in yesterday afternoon around this same hour, but Stickney had been helping another customer at the time and the man had quickly left.

The customer asked Stickney for some stamps, so the banker headed to the cashier's room to get them, not realizing that his customer was close behind and sliding a blackjack out from his pocket. In an instant, Stickney was struck and knocked unconscious. Next, the man pulled out a razor and sliced the neck of the unconscious banker, killing him.

In less than a minute, the murderer stole $4,125 worth of cash and gold and silver coins (well over $100,000 in today's dollars). With the cashier's room locked, the bandit smashed the glass window, climbed through, and walked out the bank's front entrance in the middle of downtown Somersworth.

While walking with a heavy bag slung over his shoulder, the thief was aware that he was sticking out, so he jumped a nearby fence and stashed the bag at the base of a large apple tree. After peeling off what turned out to be a fake mustache and goatee, he leapt the fence again and walked back to town to his boardinghouse on the opposite side of the street as the bank.

The man turned out to be twenty-four-year-old Joseph Kelley, who slipped his landlady $20 in back rent before heading up to his room. From his window he watched police swarm the bank after Parchie Swasey returned from her lunch hour to discover the body of her boss.

HOW THE DEED WAS DONE.

This Shows the Interior of the Bank, the Door, Window, etc. The Murderer is Striking Mr Stickney With the Blackjack.

Kelley knew the police would figure out that whoever did this was nearby and had cased the bank knowing when was the best time to strike. It would only be a matter of time before they knocked on his door. After finishing his dinner at the boarding-house, Kelley walked out with his suitcase in hand, retrieved the stolen money, stuffed the cash in his suitcase, and made for the train station, where he boarded an evening train bound for Maine to catch a connection to Canada.

Kelley was correct in his assumption the police would soon be knocking. After learning from his landlady that Kelley had come and gone several times that day, then paid his back rent and later left for the train station, police now had a prime suspect. New Hampshire law enforcement were en route to Quebec within hours.

After asking around, a local hotelkeeper said someone matching Kelley's description had paid him $10 for a woman's dress he said was for his wife in Montreal. While that's not so unusual, seeing Kelley walk out of the hotel wearing that dress a short while later was indeed strange to the hotelier.

Police tracked Kelley to a brothel in Montreal, where they found him between two sex workers still wearing the dress. He was arrested and brought back home.

Back in jail in New Hampshire, police found some drops of blood on his bowler hat, plus all of the circumstantial evidence of his timing and whereabouts. They believed they had enough evidence to convict him for murder and robbery. After checking his background, they learned that Kelley was from nearby Amesbury, Massachusetts. His troubles with the law began when he was ten years old, stealing bicycles. Clearly, his was a life of crime.

Kelley's trial began November 8, and that's when things took a strange turn. While in court, Kelley smiled through almost the entire trial, which was odd behavior for someone facing the death penalty.

It was day four of the trial when Joseph Kelley announced to the court that he was ready to plead guilty only if his hanging could be scheduled for January 16, 1898—or a little over two months later. When asked why that specific date, Kelley replied that he had a contract with the Devil that expired on January 15.

With that, the jury was dismissed. The guilty plea was accepted, and the rest of the trial focused on how mentally fit Joseph Kelley was, and what his punishment should be.

Mental health experts examined Kelley, including Dr. Charles Bancroft of the New Hampshire State Asylum for the Insane. He concluded that Kelley was "a child." The doctor went on to say, "I should place him about eight or nine years old, mentally and morally. He has the impulses and instincts of a man, but the judgment and capacity of a child of nine."

Kelley was convicted of second-degree murder and sentenced to life in prison. He was crushed that he would not hang. Folks in Somersworth didn't welcome the news either. There were several attempts to form a lynch mob to ensure that Kelley was hanged before his contract with the Devil was up, but things never came to fruition. January 15 came and went, and Old Scratch had to wait for natural causes to take Kelley and give the Devil his due.

A Haunted Lake . . . Literally

FRANCESTOWN, NEW HAMPSHIRE

What's in a name? As Shakespeare once wrote: A haunt by any other name would be just as scary. (We're paraphrasing.) Sometimes we get a lead on a story because someone had a strange experience and told another person, who told another. Over time, the haunted reputation of that location grows, and others get interested. But sometimes the name of the location is literally *Haunted* Lake.

That's the case in Francestown. Go ahead and check a map; we'll wait. When we first heard there was a body of water called "Haunted Lake," we couldn't eat or sleep until we knew why.

There are a few versions of the backstory on this haunt, and both come from the 1895 book, *History of Francestown, New Hampshire 1758 to 1891*.

One version says that when the lake was first discovered, all of the trees around the water were burned black. Maybe from a lightning strike or a small forest fire, but, either way, they say the place looked dead and ominous.

The second version of the story suggests that, back in 1741, two young men set off for Hillsborough to buy land. They decided to make camp for the night by this lake. An argument ensued and one murdered the other, burying him by the water's edge. They say the lake has been haunted ever since. Maybe there's something to that.

The lake itself isn't very large. It's about one mile measuring east to west, and a little less than one mile measuring north to south. Though we can't confirm the origins of the name for certain, we do know its reputation dates back to at least 1753.

In the *History of Francestown* book, there's a passage describing the Honorable Matthew Patten of Bedford's trip to survey the area in 1753. In his diary, he noted the following:

> Soon after darkness set in, there commenced groanings and shrieks as of a human being in distress, and these continued, most plaintive and affecting, till early morning. These chainmen were hardy fellows not accustomed to fear the face of man, but they had some superstition, and some alarm at "signs" and "bad omens," and they could not be persuaded to continue their work, even for an hour. They started at once, in the morning, for their home in Bedford. This event, of course, confirmed previous rumors that the place was "haunted," and established the name "Haunted Pond."

Fast-forward about thirty years, and a man named David Scoby bought land by the lake to construct a mill. As they were dragging logs by the water for the building, they unearthed a human skeleton. And suddenly they thought back to the story of the murdered man by the lake.

Whether Scoby's neighbors believed in ghosts or not, the lake's reputation was enhanced by Scoby's teenaged boys who would construct rafts and effigies covered in oil-soaked rags. At night they'd ignite the rags and push the raft onto the water to

frighten "liquor-laden loafers" who happened by. A few hoots and hollers from the dark woods, and those drunk neighbors high-tailed it home with a story to tell about "Haunted Lake."

Though Scoby's mill is long gone, its foundation can still be seen. The haunted reputation persists, and the "Haunted Lake" name has been official for many years.

Francestown has one other body of water in town. Its name is "Pleasant Pond." We don't care how that pond got its name.

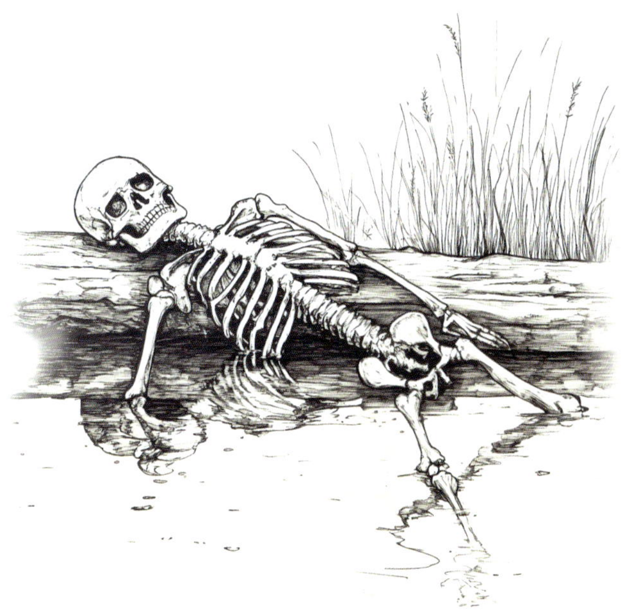

The Devil's Baked Beans

LYNDEBOROUGH, NEW HAMPSHIRE

Purgatory Falls in Lyndeborough has long been a place to visit and play. In 1889, a dance hall was constructed here, plus picnic areas and hiking trails that run along Purgatory Brook as it stretches five miles from the upper falls in the north to where it spills into Souhegan River in Milford to the south. This has been a popular place to visit ever since. As you walk along the trail next to picturesque Purgatory Falls, you may notice some strange formations in the rocks. One looks like a giant cauldron, big enough for a person to fit inside; the other is more like a half-oval impression not nearly as large. How these formations got here is a story that can't be told without the Devil.

Lyndeborough was incorporated as its own town back in 1764. The story of the strange rock formations at Purgatory Falls dates back to the town's earliest days. Back then, the town was both small and spread out. They couldn't afford a full-time preacher, so some of the local farmers took turns preaching the good word at the meetinghouse on Sundays.

The story goes that one Sunday a dashing gentleman strolled into town and approached three of the local farmers who had just preached Sunday services. The stranger claimed he'd heard great things about their sermons. Not used to flattery, the preachers smiled. That's when this gentleman invited them to lunch the following day, where fresh baked beans would be served. Now,

there isn't a New England preacher alive or dead who can resist a baked bean supper. The three preachers agreed to meet the gentleman at Purgatory Falls the next day.

When noon struck the following day, the three preachers hiked up to the falls until they saw the dashing gentleman standing on the rock stirring a steaming pot of beans. The three preachers instantly fell under a strange spell and could only stare as the stranger laughed and stirred his beans . . . beans being cooked by the very fires of hell down below.

The preachers stood frozen, and the gentleman, who everyone understood now was really the Devil, laughed and cooked the supper. But then something happened that the Devil didn't foresee. The fires of hell were so hot that they melted the rock, and soon the Devil's bean pot was sinking into the molten rock by the falls. And even the Devil's foot was sinking behind him into the melting rock. With a mighty roar the Devil screamed, then vanished. The baked beans exploded everywhere, breaking the spell on the bean-covered preachers. What remained were two strange rock formations where they say the Devil once cooked his beans.

The Ghost of Nancy Barton

CRAWFORD NOTCH, NEW HAMPSHIRE

They say the Notchland Inn is haunted. Some of the guest rooms have had strange reports. There's talk about not feeling alone in some of the rooms, or finding flowers where there were none before, or even seeing the wispy apparition of a woman gliding by before she dissipates. To figure out why this place is haunted, we need to head backward in time. The Notchland Inn was built in 1920 as a large addition to the Crawford House, which had been a tavern for over a century before that. And before there was a tavern, just up the hill in the nearby woods, a tragedy occurred that still haunts us.

In the winter of 1788, life in the White Mountains of New Hampshire was rugged, and not for the timid. In nearby Jefferson, New Hampshire, Colonel Joseph Whipple owned and ran a boardinghouse for the men who worked for him. Running the boardinghouse for Colonel Whipple was Nancy Barton.

Born and raised in Portsmouth, New Hampshire, Barton came to Jefferson several years earlier at age sixteen to work for Whipple. She was only the second white woman to pass through the Notch. The young woman did the cooking and cleaning at the boardinghouse. She worked hard, she was smart, and, because room and board was part of her payment, she managed to save almost every penny she earned. Over the years, that was adding up to a nice nest egg.

Plus, Barton was resourceful. One summer, Whipple was captured by Indians. They had the colonel tied up, and that's when Barton approached his captors with rum. They drank themselves into a stupor, which gave Barton the opportunity to cut her employer free from his ropes.

She was tough, no question. But she was also kind. And considering that she was the only eligible bachelorette in the building, the men in the boardinghouse couldn't help but be captivated by her. Different men had tried to win her affection, but they received nothing more than a polite smile.

But there was one man boarding there who did catch her eye—Jim Swindell. Swindell was just charming enough, attractive enough, and, pretty soon, Nancy Barton found herself smitten. The two talked about life in the White Mountains, about where they were from, and very quickly the talk turned to marriage.

The only problem was, Swindell confessed, that he didn't have much money saved up to start their lives together.

Barton explained how she had saved every penny for years, that she'd built up her own dowry! It was enough to give them a good start. And as a token of her faith in this wonderful man, she handed over all of her money so Swindell could keep it safe until they got to Portsmouth. So it was agreed. The couple would make their way to Portsmouth to get married and start a new life together. They would leave with the next party heading that way in a few days.

Meanwhile, Colonel Whipple was fretting over losing Nancy. She's a great cook, and he figured that no one could ever work as hard as she does. How could he replace her? So when Jim Swindell

NANCY
of JEFFERSON, N. H.
PERISHED HERE IN 1778
FOLLOWING THE WILD PATH OF THE NOTCH
FOR THIRTY MILES, IN A VAIN ATTEMPT TO
OVERTAKE HER FAITHLESS LOVER SHE PERISHED
IN A SNOW STORM BY THIS STREAM AND IS BURIED HERE.
NANCY WAS THE SECOND WOMAN TO GO THRU THE NOTCH
PASS

whispered in the colonel's ear, he nodded. And that's when the colonel sent Nancy Barton on an errand to Lancaster, the next town north of Jefferson.

Barton heard enough whispering going on at the boarding-house to suspect that something was up. She had an unsettled feeling when she left for Lancaster—one of those feelings that gnaws away at you. So, she quickened her pace on the way back. Besides, it was winter. The brisk walk warmed her up.

When Barton returned to the boardinghouse that night, she learned that her love had run off that morning with all of her money. And to make the situation even worse, Colonel Whipple was in on it! He figured if she was broke and alone, she'd have to stay. Beyond furious, Barton tied up some of her clothing into a bundle and stormed out of the boardinghouse to track down this thief.

As night fell, the frigid temps settled in, but Barton's fury kept her warm enough. A light snow began, but Nancy's blind rage kept her marching. She knew the mountains, and the Notch. She had no doubt that Jim would follow the Saco River south . . . and pretty soon she picked up his trail in the snow.

Barton walked all night until she reached a camp by a stream that spills into the Saco. There was a campfire that had been recently extinguished. Barton was exhausted, and soon had another problem.

Winter snow began to fall heavy. It was sticking to her layers of clothes and turning to ice, weighing her down. Now desperate, she looked around for any signs of twigs and branches she could use to start a fire, but it would seem the man she loved, and who she thought loved her, and who had stolen all of her money, had also taken any nearby burnable fuel. With only her anger to push her forward, she followed the snowy footprints southward, stumbling only a few feet until she reached the banks of the brook where she collapsed to the ground. The snow continued to fall as the life faded out from young Nancy Barton.

A few hours later, a search party discovered Barton's frozen corpse. They say they buried her near where they found the body.

There are stories that after Jim Swindell learned of Nancy Barton's fate, he lost his sanity and died some horrible death shortly thereafter, but that could just be us trying to find justice in a world that offered very little to Nancy Barton. What we do know is that today the name of the nearby brook is called Nancy Brook. If you follow it up the mountain it will take you to Nancy's Falls, and if you head west you'll find Nancy Pond, all under the summit of Mt. Nancy.

In 1931, a sign was placed by the hiking trail that reads:

> NANCY OF JEFFERSON, N. H. PERISHED HERE IN 1778. FOLLOWING THE WILD PATH OF THE NOTCH FOR THIRTY MILES IN A VAIN ATTEMPT TO OVERTAKE HER FAITHLESS LOVER, SHE PERISHED IN A SNOW STORM BY THE STREAM AND IS BURIED HERE. NANCY WAS THE SECOND WOMAN TO GO THRU THE NOTCH PASS.

Today, perhaps the ghost of Nancy Barton wanders down the hill to haunt the Notchland Inn in hopes that her presence will lead others to her story and maybe they won't suffer the same fate.

Madame Sherri's Castle Ruins

CHESTERFIELD, NEW HAMPSHIRE

Deep in the forest of Chesterfield sits a curved and crumbling stone staircase leading up to nowhere . . . but that wasn't always the case. Back in 1931, the stairs used to lead to Madame Antoinette Sherri's summer castle. Today, all that's left is the remains of this iconic staircase, a few foundation pillars, parts of the former fireplace chimney, and Madame Sherri's restless ghost. But who was she?

Madame Sherri was born Antoinette Bramare in 1878 in France. Destined to be onstage, she began her career as a singer, but after marrying her much younger boyfriend, Andre Riela, in 1911, the couple moved to New York City and changed their names to Andre and Antoinette Sherri. In New York, Madame Sherri began designing elaborate costumes for the Ziegfeld Follies and other notable Broadway shows of the time.

In 1927, Madame Sherri lost her young husband to illness. That summer she had the chance to visit some friends who summered in Chesterfield. She fell in love with the region and constructed her summer castle in 1931. Madame Sherri drove workers mad with her many changes during the construction, but the end result was elegant and beautiful—befitting the renowned costume designer's exquisite taste.

The summer parties thrown here were at times scandalous. Madame Sherri would wear some of her ornate Broadway costumes and greet her guests from the top of the spiral stone staircase. There were rumors that the title *Madame* was suitable in more ways than

one. Attractive men and women from New York City would come up for these parties and stay for several days at a time.

Here's the strangest thing about this eccentric woman: She didn't live in the castle. She lived in a modest farmhouse at a corner of the property.

As time went on, Madame Sherri could no longer afford her home and land. She stopped designing costumes and quickly ran out of money. By the time the castle burned down in 1962, she was a ward of Brattleboro, Vermont. She died in 1965 at the age of eighty-four. But her story doesn't end there.

It's been said that deep in the woods Madame Sherri still shows up at the top of her old staircase, ready to greet visitors who have arrived for a summer party.

The top portion of her staircase fell in 2021. We were able to photograph it before the fall. Missing from the photo is Madame Sherri's ghost.

C

America's Stonehenge

SALEM, NEW HAMPSHIRE

America's Stonehenge, or Mystery Hill as it's been called, is an enigma built of stone. The site seems to be an ancient calendar that dates back over four thousand years! We know there were people in this region four millennia ago, but those folks didn't build structures like this . . . did they? This site looks almost European or maybe even Middle Eastern in design. But people from that part of the world didn't travel to our continent thousands of years ago . . . or did they?

From the top of the hill there are various alignment stones that were used to determine specific solar and lunar events throughout the year, like solstices and equinoxes, for example. Dr. Barry Fell from Harvard University studied Mystery Hill and also found inscriptions written in Ogham, Phoenician, and Iberian Punic script.

In addition to the stones and strange writings, there are thirteen stone chambers, numerous stone walls, niches, grooves and basins. The most ominous feature on the site: a stone they call the "sacrificial table." This rock features a carved groove around the exterior that would have been used to capture blood and funnel it to one place for collection.

Acclaimed American horror writer H. P. Lovecraft, from Providence, RI, was said to be especially interested in American monolithic sites and may have visited Mystery Hill somewhere

between 1928 and the 1930s. Many Lovecraft fans attribute Mystery Hill as the inspiration and basis of his novella, *The Dunwich Horrors*—whether this is true or not is unknown.

America's Stonehenge may be the oldest still-standing structure in the United States. It was obviously a sacred site and a place for sacrifice. Perhaps that's why it's haunted today. Visitors report seeing glowing balls of light or energy flitting about the hill; others hear strange, disembodied voices echoing from the chambers by the sacrificial table.

For now, at least, this site's exact purpose remains a mystery. If the ghosts know what took place here thousands of years ago, they're keeping it to themselves.

Betty and Barney Hill's UFO Incident

LINCOLN, NEW HAMPSHIRE

On September 19, 1961, around 10:30 p.m., history was made on Route 3 in New Hampshire. Barney and Betty Hill were driving along with their dog Delsey in their 1957 Chevy Bel Air. They were heading south from their vacation at Niagara Falls and then Montreal, and were now on their way home to Portsmouth, New Hampshire. Barney Hill was Black, and Betty Hill was white, making the Hills an interracial couple, which is important to the story, given the time period. First, being an interracial couple was illegal in many US states at the time (New Hampshire was not one of them). Second, it was part of the reason for their late-night drive home. They knew they'd draw less attention in the dark and have an easier ride.

Around 10:30, Betty noticed an odd-shaped craft in the sky with flashing multicolored lights. At first Barney figured it was a jet heading toward Montreal, but then the lights turned and began descending toward them.

The Hills continued south near Franconia Notch in the White Mountains. They claim they watched this craft descend lower and lower until it passed over a restaurant and signal tower on top of Cannon Mountain and then flew out near the Old Man of the Mountain cliff face. Betty estimated that the rotating craft was bigger than the cliff profile, which was about forty feet.

About a mile south of Indian Head, the Hills say this craft quickly descended toward their car, forcing Barney to stop in the middle of the highway. There were no other cars around. The craft was now less than a hundred feet above their automobile. Barney had a pistol in his pocket, so he stepped out of his car. He used binoculars to look up and there he says he spotted several humanoid-looking figures gazing at him from the craft's windows. All of the figures but one stepped away, but one figure continued looking right at Barney. Mr. Hill claimed the creature was telepathically telling him to stay where he was and to keep observing.

The craft dropped even lower—maybe fifty feet from the ground and less than a football field away from them. Barney ran back to his car and screamed for his wife in a panic, "They're going to capture us!" At this point the Hills reported hearing a buzzing sound followed by beeps. The car vibrated and they felt a tingling sensation in their bodies. And then . . .

. . . the Hills heard those beeps and buzzing sounds again and realized they were about thirty-five miles south of where they thought they had been a moment ago. They drove up to a roadblock, stopped the car, and saw a fiery ball of light in the road. Both of their wristwatches had stopped working.

The Hills arrived home in Portsmouth around dawn. They claim they were confused, Barney felt he needed to shower to remove any possible contamination. Betty put the dress and shoes she was wearing into her closet and noticed tears in the fabric, but she didn't remember tearing her dress. She also saw some kind of

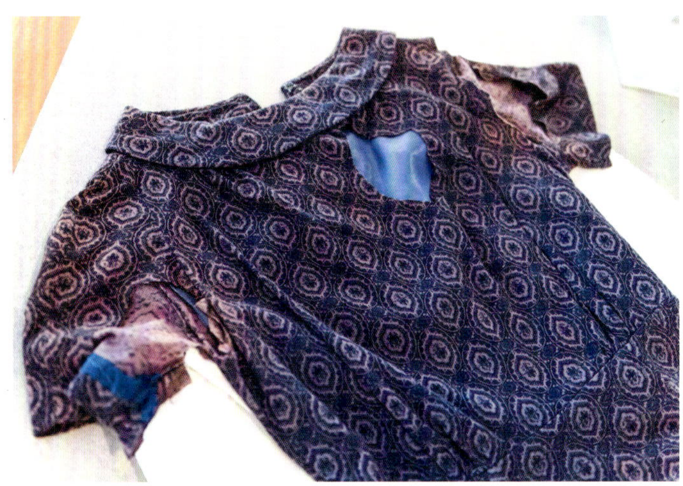

pink powder on her clothes. The trunk of their car had some concentric circles imprinted on them that hadn't been there before.

The couple wrote down everything they remembered, and the following day they phoned Pease Air Force Base in Portsmouth to report their encounter. The major who interviewed the Hills concluded that the couple had misidentified the planet Jupiter in the sky. (We'll pause here while you roll your eyes.)

In the coming days, Betty claimed to have a recurring dream in which she and Barney encountered a roadblock, their car was surrounded by men, and they were led up a ramp into a disk-shaped metallic craft. Once inside, she and Barney were separated into different rooms and examined. She remembers sitting down, a bright light, and then a physical examination of her skin, hands, feet, and body. Betty wrote down all of the details of this dream, and would later reveal them to people interested in UFOs, including US Air Force Captain Ben H. Swett. Swett also had an interest in hypnosis, and he referred the Hills to Benjamin Simon in Boston who conducted several hypnotic regressions with Betty and Barney. It's from those regressions that we get most of the details of their account.

This story really blew up in 1966 when author John G. Fuller wrote the book *The Interrupted Journey*, which propelled this experience from a regional story to an international one that people still talk about today. An interracial couple coming forward with their story opened them up to ridicule because it's a UFO encounter, but also to danger because they were an interracial couple. Yet they stuck by their story for the rest of their lives.

Their case now has some official state recognition. There's a historic marker detailing the event outside of Indian Head Resort in Lincoln, near the couple's original driving route. And if you like your memorials a little more gaudy, there's the Irving Express Gas Station off exit 33 on I-93 with a painted wall showing your typical gray alien standing on the road with a sign that reads:

First close encounter of the third kind.
Betty and Barney Hill September 19, 1961.

Rhode Island

Born: May 29, 1790

New England's (and America's, for that matter) smallest state still packs a big punch. For one, the state had the longest name in the nation for most of its life: *State of Rhode Island and Providence Plantations* was the official moniker right up until the year 2020 when they downsized it to just *Rhode Island*. With almost four hundred miles of coastline, the Ocean State knows a thing or two about the sea, lighthouses, and the many dangers that come with living on or near the water.

People from Rhode Island don't mind sticking out in a crowd either. Just ask former Rhode Island Governor and Civil War General Ambrose Burnside. He once grew the strangest formation of facial hair: not quite a beard, but not clean-shaven either. It's not (much of) an overreach to say that without General Burnside, Elvis Presley would never have worn sideburns . . . *thankyaverymuch*.

Rhode Islanders also know about vampires, werewolves, ghosts, and all manner of weirdness that lurks on the land. They know about making grand gestures for love, and the heartbreak that can follow. The state may be small, but their history and high strangeness are big.

The Legendary Fountain of Benefit Street

PROVIDENCE, RHODE ISLAND

Standing in front of the Providence Athenaeum, next to the sidewalk out front, sits an ornate stone fountain with magical abilities to transport you . . . at least that's what they say.

The fountain project was conceived by a wealthy widow named Ann Eddy Richmond back in 1873. Civic work was nothing new for Richmond; she and her family toiled tirelessly to further the cause of freedom of religious belief, access to education, science, and justice. She also fully supported the temperance movement (nobody's perfect).

Richmond used her wealth and influence to fund various public works, to bring professors to town to lecture, and to do anything else she could to make the world a better place.

One hot day in 1873 on Benefit Street, Richmond took note of sweaty, thirsty people walking by her neighborhood. There was no place for the public to get some free water, so she decided to do something about that.

Richmond advanced the handsome sum of $600, hired some fancy architects from Ware and Van Brunt in Boston, and soon ground was broken on this new fountain, right in front of the Providence Athenaeum.

The fountain was made in a Gothic Revival style. Carved across the arch read the words: A.D. 1873. COME HITHER EVERY ONE THAT THIRSTETH. The line across the top is from Scripture. Isaiah Chapter 55 verse 1: "The Lord says come hither, every one that thirsteth. Come, thou who hath no money to buy grain, eat." Richmond loved the idea that the Athenaeum can quench your intellectual thirst, while this fountain can quench your body's physical thirst.

Part of the reason Richmond had the fountain built was that she thought if maybe more people had free access to water, they might drink less beer (leaving more beer for the rest of us).

With the new fountain installed, a steady stream of water spilled into a small bowl before draining below. Any passersby could walk up with their own cup or use the communal bronze cup placed there (*ewwww*) and drink. This was Providence's first public water fountain.

Which brings us to the magical qualities of the fountain. Some say it's cursed, that those who drink from it will never leave Providence. In 1986, one local man was walking to Brown University for his admissions interview, and took a drink from the fountain. He later heard about the curse that those who drink from it never leave Providence. He said that after graduating from Brown he was in a motorcycle accident and couldn't take the job in Alaska he wanted. So he attended grad school at Brown and never left Providence.

Sure, that's just one story of countless people who drank from the fountain. But the second version of the legend is that those who drink will find themselves magically transported back to Providence . . . which is exactly where the fountain already resides . . . which means the legend holds true 100 percent of the time without exception.

The Cumberland Vampire

CUMBERLAND, RHODE ISLAND

When you think of vampires, it's easy to let your mind wander to Hollywood's notion of what that means . . . whether attractive teenagers who sparkle in the sunlight, or sinister people who can turn into bats and suck your blood, or the Nosferatu character if you're more old-fashioned. When Bram Stoker published his horror masterpiece *Dracula* in 1897, he drew a line in the sand forever delineating between our modern vampire and what they had been for centuries before.

Traditional vampires are walking corpses who drain the vitality and life force from those they attack. Vampires were most often victims of a plague. New England has had its share of these vampires and its share of plagues. But chief among the illnesses that led to vampirism was consumption, also known as the "wasting disease," and medically referred to as tuberculosis.

Tuberculosis is caused by a bacteria that infects the lungs and eats away at you from the inside. It could kill some people in a matter of weeks, while for others it took months and even years, and some people lived with it for decades. Though people two centuries ago understood contagion, consumption seemed beyond chance. Why would it wipe out one entire family and completely spare another? When medical science doesn't have a satisfying answer as to why this sickness was hunting you and your family, and when your preacher's explanation of "God's will" doesn't sit right with you either, folklore always offers an alternative: You're the victim of a vampire. Find the vampire, and you may break the spell.

Just off Route 120 in Cumberland sits Rhode Island Historic Cemetery Number 17, a tiny square of land with a smattering of headstones and fieldstones whose inscriptions have been mostly lost to time. However, among the dead lie the mortal remains of a suspected vampire.

During a Cumberland town meeting in February 1796, Mr. Stephen Staples approached the council with a request unlike any they'd heard before. The meeting's minutes have survived and help tell the story:

> Mr. Stephen Staples of Cumberland appeared before this council and prayed that he might have liberty granted unto him to dig up the body of his daughter Abigail Staples, late of Cumberland, single woman, deceased, in order to try an experiment on Lavinia Chace, wife of Stephen Chace, which said Lavinia was sister to said Abigail, deceased. Which being duly considered it is voted and resolved the said Stephen Staples have liberty to dig up the body of said Abigail, deceased, and after trying this experiment as aforesaid that he bury the body of the said Abigail in a decent manner.

Abigail Staples died from consumption. Her sister Lavinia was also afflicted, and her health was declining. Though a medical doctor may have suggested there was little that could be done for Lavinia, and perhaps the preacher suggested prayer, others told

Stephen Staples there's a remedy: If you find the vampire, you may have a chance to break the spell.

The vampire was usually a family member who died before the afflicted—in this case, Abigail Staples. If you exhume the corpse, you can look for signs that the deceased may be a vampire—signs like decomposition not being as far along as it should be, or perhaps the body had moved in the casket, or if you cut the chest cavity open, there may be liquid blood in the heart. At that point you disrupt the suspected vampire. You may burn the corpse, or cut the vital organs out, burn them, and mix the ashes into an elixir to feed to the sick, or decapitate the vampire, or flip the body upside down. The point is to take some kind of long-shot chance because Stephen Staples was scared of losing another daughter, and in that desperate time he requested of the town permission to dig up Abigail and do something that sounds barbaric and backwoods by today's standards, but it at least gave Staples some peace knowing he had truly tried everything.

The town records don't reveal the outcome of his experiment, but the suspected vampire Abigail Staples is indeed buried somewhere in the tiny cemetery off Route 120.

Stephen Smith's Heartbreak House

LINCOLN, RHODE ISLAND

If you asked wealthy eccentric Stephen Hopkins Smith what he named his 1814 mansion, he'd tell you, "The House That Love Built." Ask the locals who know his story what they call it, and they'll tell you, "Heartbreak House."

In 1810, Smith was a young twenty-something Quaker with a love of plants. If it grew, flowered, crept, crawled, blossomed, or was simply the right shade of green, he wanted it. He collected and cultivated all kinds of flowers and plants. Smith was also a romantic at heart and soon fell in love with a Providence socialite. But they came from different worlds. She was from a wealthy family, and he was but a humble Quaker from rural Rhode Island. She could only ever live in the finest of homes, and what could he provide her?

That's when something incredibly lucky happened to young Stephen. He turned to a game of chance. Not the most Christian thing he could do, but desperate times and all that. Lotteries had been around for at least two thousand years. Even in early America, many church and civic projects were funded by lotteries. You could argue that a lot of early America was built by gamblers. So Stephen took a chance . . . and won the kingly sum of $40,000.

The Smith family owned 249 acres of farmland off Great Road. Stephen took some of his winnings and constructed a stately mansion right across the street from his childhood home. When finished, the two-and-a-half-story mansion featured windows topped by granite lintels, wooden pillars, and ten rooms with a fireplace in each room. He also built a textile mill, called Smith Manufacturing Company, right down the road from his mansion, and surely with all that money, and now a business and a mansion, he'd be a baron worthy of the beautiful Providence socialite he'd been wooing for years.

As Smith brought the woman in a buggy down Great Road to see the house that love had built just for her, she said, "My, what a beautiful house, but who would ever want to live way out here in the wilderness?" Heartbroken and dejected, Smith brought her back to Providence. He never married, and he never lived in the mansion.

His business didn't fare much better than his heart. His textile mill couldn't compete and soon went out of business. With no love and no business, he turned back to the first object of his affection: plants. He funded the Rhode Island Horticultural Society, he traveled, he planted lush gardens on his property, and he lived in the shadow of "Heartbreak House" until his death in 1857.

His obituary summed him up thusly: "Many men of larger mental development, more honored with office and more favored of fortune than Stephen Hopkins Smith, have gone down to the grave; yet there are few who could compare with him in warmth and affection, benignity of disposition, or genuine goodness of heart."

Today his mansion is known as Hearthside House and still offers a few surprises like a heart-shaped reflection that will tug at your heartstrings.

Should Have Been the Wife of Simeon Palmer

LITTLE COMPTON, RHODE ISLAND

The epitaph reads: IN MEMORY OF ELIZABETH WHO *SHOULD* HAVE BEEN THE WIFE OF SIMEON PALMER WHO DIED AUGUST 4, 1776 IN THE 64TH YEAR OF HER AGE.

The statement conjures up an image of a woman who pined away for a man named Simeon until her death, her love obviously unrequited. But the true story is much stranger.

The deepest roots of this story date back to the early 18th century to a Reverend Richard Billings who preached in Little Compton's first church. The preacher was dynamic, folks liked him, but he had his eccentricities. For one, he preached about self-care, including praying daily, living cleanly, and taking care of your body. That included eating well, and the good reverend's food source included a steady diet of cat meat.

Yes, *that* kind of cat. He raised and bred cats for food.

From here we jump ahead to 1745 to meet twenty-one-year-old Simeon Palmer. Palmer came from a prominent family in town and was considered one of the most eligible bachelors around. That's when Lydia Dennis caught his eye. The two courted, were married, and began their family together.

By the summer of 1751, Lydia and Simeon were living the dream until a hot summer's day when Simeon overdid the

In Memory of
ELIZABETH who
Should have been the
Wife of Mr.
SIMEON PALMER
who died Augt 14th
1776 in the 94th Year
of her Age.

farmwork under the scorching sun. Suddenly, Simeon collapsed with sunstroke, which can be fatal. Lydia dragged her husband into the shade and cooled him with water and damp rags.

Simeon recovered, but he was never the same. It was clear he'd suffered some brain damage. After the sunstroke, he was a little disheveled and wide-eyed, and paid a lot more attention in church. Pretty soon, he announced to his family that he was going to change the way they ate. Like Reverend Billings, they were going to start eating cat meat. His wife, Lydia, wasn't pleased about her husband's decision, but she did her best to choke down her new diet.

Whether it was the new diet of cat meat or dealing with this new version of her husband—we can't be sure—we do know that Lydia died just a couple of years later in December 1754, at thirty-six years of age.

Simeon didn't waste too much time mourning the loss of his wife. By spring he was on the prowl and soon discovered Elizabeth Mortimer. Ten years his senior, Elizabeth had never been married. When this younger, wealthy man came calling, she jumped at the chance (looking right past his quirky behavior and strange diet). The two were wed on September 5, 1755.

Two years later, the couple welcomed their first child into the world, a daughter named Lydia. Though it would never fly in today's society, it wasn't uncommon back then to name a child after your dead wife.

Not long after the birth of their daughter, Elizabeth could take no more of living with her husband. Maybe it was the cats, maybe it was his strange behavior, probably it was both, but Elizabeth took their daughter back to her parents' house permanently.

However, Simeon and Elizabeth didn't get divorced. In fact, Simeon visited Elizabeth each Saturday. He brought his clothes that needed mending, and while she worked they'd chat about life and then he'd leave until the following week.

This continued for almost two decades until August 14, 1775, when sixty-four-year-old Elizabeth Palmer passed away. Her family could scarcely afford the burial, and that's when Simeon Palmer stepped in to help pay for all of the costs. His only condition: He gets to write the epitaph. The Mortimer family agreed, and Elizabeth was buried right next to Simeon's first wife, under a stone that reads "Should have been the wife of Simeon Palmer."

Which gives Simeon the last word on what kind of wife he thought she was (or wasn't).

She Laughed Herself to Death

NEWPORT, RHODE ISLAND

There's little we can add to what's already in this short article that made the rounds in many 1878 newspapers across the nation. However, seeking a medical opinion, we reached out to cardiologist Dr. Dan Steinhaus who did his medical residency in Boston, and asked him the burning question: Can you die from laughing? His response sent chills to the deepest, darkest parts of our souls. "It's possible to die from pretty much *any*thing," Dr. Steinhaus said. This was especially frightening news because we do *things* all the time!

Knowing nothing other than what's in the article, Dr. Steinhaus could only speculate. Could she have laughed and then choked? Could her laughter have triggered a cardiac arrest or a stroke from a preexisting condition? We'll never know. But we're taking no chances. We've sworn off laughter forever.

—Joshua Walker, of Newport, R. I., recently purchased a quantity of pork and taking it home proceeded to salt it down. His wife soon after discovered that he had been trying to make brine with white sugar. She was seized with a fit of laughter which continued for several minutes, when she suddenly expired. Mrs. Walker was only twenty years old and had been but recently married.

An Explosion Jarred Some Passengers

PROVIDENCE, RHODE ISLAND

Imagine yourself riding along in an electric streetcar full of people from Providence toward the Massachusetts state line. The day is stifling hot. Windows are open, which helps, but only a little. The heat is making you drowsy . . . it's okay to doze just a little . . . Suddenly: *BOOM!* An explosion rocks the car!

Are you under attack?! Was someone shot?! Did the streetcar just explode?! And why are you covered in slimy goo that looks and feels almost like clam chowder?

It turns out the cause of the explosion that one witness described as "if a battery of artillery had been fired" was caused by a jar of yeast a young man in the back of the car was carrying. The heat caused the yeast to react, releasing gas that was trapped in the sealed jar until the vessel couldn't contain it any longer and then . . . *BOOM!*

The article goes on to describe the reaction of one of the male passengers, ". . . a man up forward felt his collar wabble in back. He ran his fingers around there and brought them back with this sticky material on them. He smelled of the fluid and then swore volubly and like an old-fashioned pirate . . . The man with the ruined collar continued to raise his voice in language deep and picturesque. His vocabulary was wonderful."

Cranston's Headless Corpse

CRANSTON, RHODE ISLAND

When you think of the word *ghoul*, today the image of a ghost or goblin might come to mind, but during the 19th century, *ghoul* referred to a grave robber. Grave robbing was big business back then. The deceased may have been buried with fancy and expensive jewelry or fine clothes. Sometimes teeth had gold in them and on them. Digging up a grave to yank some teeth may just be worth a ghoul's time. Ghouls were enough of a problem that cemeteries employed night watchmen to keep the dead buried. At least, the high-end boneyards employed guards. Others didn't keep watch over the dead, especially if they figured these were poor folks with nothing worth stealing. But there were other reasons ghouls might prey on the grave of someone who died penniless.

On November 15, 1883, Mary Wood of Coventry, Rhode Island, hired an undertaker to travel to the Cranston Hospital for the Insane and exhume grave #599. Lying below was her brother, Caleb R. Brown. He was an inmate in the hospital who had passed away about four months earlier on July 2. He was only twenty-five years old at the time of his passing. Since no family was there at the time to claim his mortal remains, he was buried among hundreds of other inmates who perished at the hospital with no family to offer them anything better than a number. When Ms. Wood learned the fate of her brother, she petitioned the superintendent to retrieve Caleb's body and transfer the remains to Crompton, Rhode Island, to be reinterred next to his father. This kind of request was not unusual for the superintendent, and permission was granted. What was unusual was what they found when they began to dig.

As the undertaker's workers began to exhume the body, they found some splintered pieces of wood. Then they found two large stones weighing close to fifty pounds each. Something was amiss. When graves are dug—especially just a few months earlier—if any large stones are found, they are removed. And the splintered wood? Something was definitely wrong. When they reached the coffin, they discovered a sight that left them all aghast. The coffin had indeed been broken into, and the body of Caleb Brown was still inside, but his head was nowhere to be found.

The Cranston Hospital superintendent was beside himself. He ordered several of the other nearby graves exhumed for any sign of ghouls, but those coffins were intact. Brown's head was never seen again. The November 19, 1883 *Boston Globe* covered the story and could only offer gruesome speculation as to what had happened. They believed the ghouls came for the body of Caleb Brown when he was freshly buried. They were likely working for a medical school or doctor who wanted a mental patient specimen. Since it takes a lot of time and commotion to dig up a grave illegally, professional ghouls would often just dig a small hole over the head of the coffin to save time. Once they cracked open the top, a large fishhook type of implement could be shoved under the chin and into the skull. Then, with a rope, a

horse could drag a body up through that hole and out of the grave. As you can imagine, there could be breakage. In this case, they believe, Brown's head came clean off while his body remained. What the ghouls wanted with only a damaged head, we can only wonder.

The Woonsocket Werewolf

WOONSOCKET, RHODE ISLAND

Woonsocket was first settled in the 1820s. It quickly grew into an industrial town where mills popped up along the Blackstone River. With so many mills and factories, there were lots of jobs available. Many French-Canadians came down from Quebec and settled here looking for work. By 1913, Woonsocket had the sixth-largest concentration of French or French-Canadian people in the United States.

The French-Canadians brought their work ethic, their religion, and their superstitions and beliefs in monsters—specifically the *loup-garou*, or werewolf. The *loup-garou* is a cursed person who brought this monstrous affliction upon themselves. It was seen as God's punishment.

The story of the Woonsocket werewolf dates back to the 1860s. With so many mills and factories along the Blackstone River, workdays were often as long as the sun shone. Workers started early in the morning and toiled until the sun set. By the end of the day, folks were dog-tired.

The French-Canadians were often devoutly religious too. Sundays were all about church and family. The problem was that there weren't enough churches for the Woonsocket faithful. Catholics had to travel many miles for church services.

A local priest lobbied parishioners to build a new church in Woonsocket. He begged and pleaded, but the people of

Woonsocket had little energy after their long workweeks, they had little money to spare, and their animals had to work their own homesteads. They couldn't be spared even for the church.

So this priest prayed. He said novenas to the Virgin Mary. Finally, his prayers were answered when the priest woke up one morning to find a beast of a horse as black as night with glowing red eyes standing outside of his cottage. The Virgin Mary appeared before the priest and told him this beast of burden would help build the church, but the priest must never remove the horse's bridle, or it would be gone forever.

The priest agreed and construction finally began on a new church. This horse could do the work of five or six horses. The priest told the foreman to never remove the horse's bridle or else. The foreman agreed. Though the priest was grateful for the help from this powerful horse . . . something about his glowing red eyes made everyone uncomfortable. Pretty soon, the priests suspected this horse was the Devil himself, placed under some kind of spell by the Virgin Mary.

Work progressed on the church at a quick pace. In just a few weeks, the walls were up, timber was set in place for the roof and steeple, and the priest was grateful that the Woonsocket faithful would soon have a church to call their own. But one day, the foreman was too sick to work. So he told one of the other workers to take over. He also passed along the warning about never removing the horse's bridle. The worker nodded and got back to work.

The worker led the horse out to Fairmont Hills in Woonsocket near the Blackstone River to pick up some more stones for the construction. Being a hot day, the worker saw no harm in letting the horse take a quick drink from the water. He took the bridle off for just a minute when suddenly a fiery chasm opened up in the ground! The horse morphed into a demonic beast with bat-like wings, and roared as he slipped back underground.

The worker stood there stunned for only a moment until a violent transformation overtook him. Hair grew out from all over his body as his hands and feet turned into paws with claws. For his sin, this worker was made into a *loup-garou*—a werewolf!

Back at the church, the priest soon learned what had happened. By the time he made his way back to Fairmont Hills, he could see that the chasm was now just a dark cave near the Blackstone River. And the *loup-garou* was nowhere to be found.

This area was now cursed. People who knew the story avoided the new cave whenever possible. Folks coming by on horseback claimed their horse would only get so close and then refuse to go any farther. Dark storm clouds would form just over this part of the woods. And pretty soon, the cave earned the ominous moniker: the Devil Hole.

It didn't take long for word of the *loup-garou* and the Devil Hole to spread throughout the French-Canadian community in Woonsocket. Some of the more sinful among the town came to the Devil Hole to make an unholy pact with Satan. The word is they got what they asked for, but the price was not only their soul, but that they too became a *loup-garou*.

The Haunting of Conimicut Lighthouse

WARWICK, RHODE ISLAND

Before the days of light automation, back when keepers and often their families had to live and work in a lighthouse, one of the greatest challenges was to maintain your sanity.

Nowhere was that more true than in Conimicut Light, just off the coast of Warwick. Located about half a mile off the shore of Conimicut Point, a lighthouse was first placed here in 1868 just after the Civil War to protect the ships navigating the sometimes shallow shoals in these waters. In 1883, a more modern lighthouse, built of cast iron, replaced the original light. It was fifty-eight feet tall and included the keeper's quarters. The structure sits on a pile of rocks in the ocean with no land around it. Imagine living there with a family and two young, energetic boys?

That was the situation in June of 1922. Ellsworth Smith was the lighthouse keeper back then. He lived in the lighthouse with his thirty-year-old wife, Nellie, and their two young sons, Russell, aged two, and Ellsworth Jr., aged five.

Living in the small quarters with young boys proved to be tedious and cramped, especially for Nellie. Though they had been living there for about a year, Nellie was going stir-crazy. She asked her husband if they could rent a small place on shore where she and the children could live while he was at the lighthouse, but Ellsworth knew they couldn't afford it on his meager salary.

Each day, Nellie grew more despondent. She'd even threatened suicide, but Ellsworth figured it was just a phase. They didn't intend to live there forever, just until they could save enough money to make their next move.

The better the weather, the worse it was for Nellie's depression. From the lighthouse the family could see Rocky Point Amusement Park with all of its rides, music, laughter, and excitement. And Nellie and the kids had to watch from a distance. They may as well have lived on the moon.

On Saturday, June 10, 1922, Ellsworth announced that he would take the boat to shore to get supplies and return by evening. He'd left Nellie in charge of tending to the lighthouse, which wasn't asking much, considering the fine weather.

Nellie watched her husband row the boat to shore. As he neared the coast, she turned back inside the lighthouse and removed some poison from their supply cabinet. She gathered her two young sons, and told them she had some candy for them. Her youngest son swallowed the bitter tablets he was given, Nellie also swallowed some, but her eldest son spit them out.

Russell soon fell unconscious. Nellie, though weakened, lifted his body and placed him on their kitchen table before walking to her bed to lie down.

By the time Ellsworth returned to the lighthouse around 6:00 p.m., he was shocked to see Russell lying lifeless on their kitchen table. Then he found his wife's body lying in bed. Ellsworth Jr. was groaning in the corner, still alive, though very sick.

Life on Lighthouse Lonely, Mother Poisons Self and Children

Providence, R. I., June 10.—Mrs. Nellie Smith, 30, wife of Ellsworth Smith, keeper of Conimicut Light in Narragansett Bay, administered poison tablets to her two sons, two and five years old respectively, and then took poison herself. The youngest boy and mother are dead and the oldest boy is in a critical condition.

After a year of desolate existence in the lighthouse, Mrs. Smith had grown morose and despondent. Several times she had importuned her husband to take her away from the place.

Ellsworth scooped up his son, rowed for shore as fast as he could, and got his son medical help. Thankfully, the child survived and fully recovered, but the reputation of Conimicut Lighthouse did not.

The police recovered the bodies of the Smith family, but Ellsworth could never bring himself to go back. However, duties still called. Another keeper and his family moved in, all the while living in the same cramped space that proved too much for Nellie.

The lighthouse's haunted reputation was sealed. The ghost of Nellie became a fixture. She would stand in doorways at night, or glide through the building as a reminder of the horrific past. Though no one felt threatened by her presence, they were plenty spooked.

By the 1960s, the lighthouse was taken over by the Coast Guard and the light was automated. With no more people living and working inside the lighthouse, we're left with only the stories and the beacon that shines just offshore.

The Burning Beast of Glocester

GLOCESTER, RHODE ISLAND

In early February 1896, Glocester local Neil Hopkins was walking home after a day's work on Dandelion Hill. As he approached a dark section of the road, a loud noise seized his attention.

Hopkins heard some kind of large animal lurking in the nearby woods. He snapped his head to look, and saw a sight he would never forget. Hopkins said in an interview:

> It was as big as an elephant! It seemed to be all a-fire. It had a hot breath. There was a metallic sound, like the clanking of steel against steel. The beast didn't seem to be strong in the wind, for it chased me only a short distance and then plunged off into the woods. I could hear the dead branches and twigs cracking under the heavy tramp. And I'm certain the beast had no tail.

Hopkins's encounter started a buzz after it was reported in the newspapers. Speculation ran wild. Could it have been a cow? Others recalled that a circus bear had gotten loose and did scare a few farmers the previous fall, but that bear was long gone, right? Those who knew the old stories believed Hopkins had seen the Burning Beast of Glocester.

Tales of the Burning Beast dated back another half century to 1838 to when a local ne'er-do-well named Albert Hicks went searching for buried treasure.

Albert Hicks grew up in nearby Foster, Rhode Island, but left home at the age of fifteen to begin his life of crime in Norwich, Connecticut. In his travels he'd heard plenty of stories of buried pirate treasure. After escaping from a Connecticut jail, he made his way to Glocester. In the summer of 1838, he overheard a local whispering about some Spanish doubloons unearthed on the Page Farm in Glocester. Hicks made the connection to the legends of Captain Kidd's lost treasure. Captain Kidd plundered a fortune in the late 1600s and allegedly buried plenty of his bounty. Kidd was said to have a friend in the Rhode Island pirate Thomas Paine.

When Captain Kidd was on the run, he anchored in Jamestown, Rhode Island, and asked Paine to help him hide some of his bounty because the authorities were closing in. That treasure could be anywhere in Rhode Island. Or split up into multiple locations. So, acting on the lead of Spanish doubloons on the Page Farm, Albert Hicks gathered a crew.

They snuck onto the Page Farm at night and began to dig. They were so focused on their digging, and how they were going to spend their imminent fortune, that they didn't notice a beast closing in on them . . . until they heard a mighty roar! Hicks described what he saw:

> It was a large animal, with staring eyes as big as pewter bowls. The eyes looked like balls of fire. When it breathed as it went by, flames came out of its mouth and nostrils, scorching the brush in its path. It was as big as a cow, with dark wings on each side like a bat's. It had spiral horns like a ram's, as big around as a stovepipe. Its feet were formed like a duck's and measured a foot and a half across. The body was covered with scales as big as clam shells, which made a rattling noise as the beast moved along. The scales flopped up and down. The thing had lights on its sides like those shining through a tin lantern.

Those who believed Hicks think it lent some credence to the treasure being buried at the Page Farm. Clearly this monster was the guardian of the booty. Others think maybe Hicks found some of Captain Kidd's gold and summoned this beast to protect the site until he could return for the rest. Either way, we have two documented sightings of a strange beast lurking around the Glocester area sixty years apart, which makes us wonder if the gold and the monster might still be there.

The Floating Heads of the Kickemuit River

WARREN, RHODE ISLAND

The Kickemuit River is short, but what it lacks in length and breadth, it makes up for in gruesome haunted history. Along the water's banks in Warren, some unlucky passersby have seen the anguished faces of eleven severed heads floating above the water by the river's edge. Those heads serve as a warning to us all that trespassing means war.

King Philip's War was the bloodiest conflict per capita in both British and American history—meaning both sides lost the greatest percentage of population compared to any other war. "King Philip" was the name the British gave to Metacomet, a Pokanoket Sachem. Metacomet saw a bleak future for his people considering how many colonists were arriving from England and how many Native peoples were being displaced. So Metacomet formed an alliance with other tribes in the region, and vowed to defend their homeland from the British.

This war got its bloody start right here on the banks of the Kickemuit.

On June 20, 1675, a group of Pokanoket natives from their nearby village of Montaup looted and burned the homes of some English settlers living on the banks of the river. Three days later, more houses were ransacked, then set ablaze. After all, to the Pokanoket, these settlers were trespassing. And by the spring of 1675, there was no end in sight to how many people would keep coming from Europe.

Of course, on the other side of the equation, the colonists also intended to fight for their new homeland. One settler, John Salisbury, took up his musket and fired at a Pokanoket warrior in retaliation. The warrior survived the shot, but blood had been spilled, and now the Pokanoket were furious.

Later that day, Salisbury, along with ten other settlers, was ambushed and killed near Swazey Corner. Every colonist in the region was rattled, but not nearly as shaken as they were a week later when they found the heads of all eleven settlers mounted on poles on the banks of the Kickemuit.

Kickemuit translates to "at the large spring," which is fitting because, from this location and this event, an awful war burst forth. King Philip's War would ravage southern New England for the next three years, leaving both sides changed forever. Close to 70 percent of the Native population was either killed, starved, or run off their land, and more than 10 percent of the colonists were killed.

Today, a small stone monument marks the place where the men were slain, where the bloodiest war began, and where ghostly severed heads still make an appearance from time to time to forever haunt us, and maybe remind us of the awesome price of what can happen when you can't live in harmony with your neighbors.

The Bell Still Tolls at the Ram Tail Factory

FOSTER, RHODE ISLAND

"Life how short! Eternity how long!" So reads the epitaph on the grave of Peleg Walker. Though he took his own life on May 19, 1822, eternity may be exactly how long his restless spirit intends to wander the ruins of the former Ram Tail Factory, lying deep in the woods of Foster.

Ram Tail holds the distinct honor of being Rhode Island's official haunt, according to the 1885 Rhode Island State Census. How it earned that distinction is the story of Peleg Walker and a family business.

In 1813, William Potter broke ground on a water-powered mill. To get enough capital, Potter brought in his son Olney, his brother-in-law Jonathan Ellis, and his two sons-in-law Marvin Round and Peleg Walker as partners. Pooling their money, they purchased six acres of land next to the Ponaganset River.

There they built the Foster Woolen Manufactory—a fulling mill that processed raw wool into cloth and yarn. By the end of the workday, the floor would be covered with little curls of cut-off wool that resembled a ram's tail. The nickname stuck.

Each day Peleg Walker unlocked the mill in the morning to ring the work bell, and each night he locked up. The business prospered; however, Peleg Walker got himself into financial trouble in 1822. When he went to his father-in-law for help, William Potter refused to help him, and Walker was told to turn in his keys the following day, as he'd no longer be a partner as of midnight.

Walker was overheard saying, "The next time you take these keys from me, it will be out of the pocket of a dead man."

True to his word, that night Peleg Walker locked up the mill, but remained on the inside. He waited until late that night when he was no longer a partner, and he slit his own throat with cutting shears. His body was found the next morning. Peleg was thirty-five years old.

For years after, locals would hear the work bell tolling late at night, only to find the factory empty. In more extreme lore about the factory, some workers came in to find the waterwheel spinning against the flow of water. Everyone knew the place was haunted to the point where it made the census as a footnote.

After the mill closed in 1850, the building sat abandoned, but not empty. And a ghost, assumed to be that of Peleg Walker, has been reported walking the grounds carrying a lantern ever since.

When the structure burned down to its foundation in 1873, some thought the fire would cleanse the place of spirits, but that didn't work. To this day, the phantom bell still tolls deep in the woods, and Walker still oversees the ruins of the business that was once partly his.

Mr.
PELEG WALKER
died May 19th, 1822
in his 35th
year.
Life how short!
Eternity how long!

The Moaning Bones of Mt. Tom

EXETER, RHODE ISLAND

At 430 feet above sea level, Mt. Tom has the distinction of being Rhode Island's highest point. Though that's tiny compared to any mountain anywhere, if we're to believe the legends, what Mt. Tom lacks in size it makes up for in haunted lore. If you find yourself hiking the woods of Mt. Tom, near the remains of an old cemetery, you may just hear the disembodied moan of a murdered man still crying out for justice all these years later.

The first time the story of the Moaning Bones of Mt. Tom appeared in print was in the 1937 *WPA Guide to Rhode Island*. However, the story had been circulating for many decades prior.

The story goes that long ago there was a small farmhouse on the slope of Mt. Tom. The only two people living inside were a farmer and his teenaged daughter. One day, a peddler came along to sell his wares. The farmer wasn't interested in buying anything, so the peddler struck a deal. If the farmer would feed him dinner and give him a place to sleep for the night, the peddler would sharpen all of the farmer's knives. The farmer agreed.

After dinner, the peddler got to work on the farmer's knives. After cleaning up from dinner, the daughter bid her father and their guest goodnight and went to her bedroom. Just as she was falling asleep, the girl heard a loud commotion. After walking out to see what happened, she found the peddler in a pool of his own blood. Without a word or reaction, the daughter began to rifle through the peddler's bag to see what she could claim for herself.

While his daughter took what wasn't hers, the farmer began pulling stones out from the hearth and digging a hole in order to hide the peddler's body. Once the body was covered, and the last hearthstone put back into place, the farmer grew suspicious of his daughter . . . what if she talked about what happened in their home? The farmer grabbed one of his freshly sharpened knives, squeezed his daughter's cheeks until her tongue came out, then he sliced off her tongue so she could never speak of the brutal murder that had taken place there.

After years passed, the farmer and his daughter moved on, and the old farmhouse slowly rotted away as nature reclaimed what was always hers. But the bones of that peddler remain where they've been since he was unjustly murdered all those years ago. And they say you can still hear the moans when you walk by the grounds where he lies buried.

Though we don't know the exact location where the old farmhouse stood, today there is a sign in the woods designating the place where historical cemetery 65 is. There are no headstones or fieldstones marking any graves, just the sign placed by the Rhode Island Commission on Historic Cemeteries. However, a few miles to the north, there are ruins of an old hearth and chimney in the woods of Arcadia. We weren't brave enough to bring a shovel and dig.

The Narragansett Rune Stone

NORTH KINGSTOWN, RHODE ISLAND

We love mysteries that shake up the history books. By now, it's well established that Christopher Columbus was *not* the first European in the New World. Now on display on dry land for all to see, the Narragansett Rune Stone is a 2.5-ton rock carved with strange markings. The runic symbols hold a mystery, and the rock itself has seen more than its share of controversy.

Back in 1938, a hurricane ripped through the region, forever altering the coastline of Pojac Point in North Kingstown. After the hurricane, during the lowest part of low tide, a rock made an appearance. While most rocks in the surf don't cause a stir, this one did because of strange markings that had been carved into the rock's face. Clearly the marks were some foreign and strange language and they had been carved by a human hand.

By the 1980s, the stone caught the attention of the New England Antiquities Research Association (NEARA), which identified the markings as Nordic runes that could date back between AD 600 and 1000. In the spring of 1991, Suzanne O. Carlson wrote in the *New England Antiquities Research Association Journal* that the letters translate to the Nordic word, *Skraumligr*, which means "screaming river." It was thought to be named for a river in Iceland. The theory is that Vikings came here over a thousand years ago and carved the name of where they were from into a rock by the water.

All the while, the legend of this rock only grew. Word began to circulate, bringing in the curious to a swanky beach and offending some of the local homeowners. They didn't like too many outsiders coming around at low tide to look at their rock. Tensions were high.

Tensions grew until sometime between July and August of 2012. That's when someone stole the 2.5-ton rock during low tide.

This is not the kind of move you pull off by offering a few buddies some pizza and beer to help you. This took power equipment. And, suddenly, the state of Rhode Island cared very much about their Pojac Point rock. People around the state were buzzing about the stolen rock. For eight months it was missing, until the state received an anonymous tip as to where it could be found.

Once recovered, the stone was then moved to the University of Rhode Island's School of Oceanography in Narragansett for study, and then moved once again to its new permanent home in Library Park in North Kingstown, for all to see and ponder anytime they liked.

The Northern Rhode Island UFO Flap of 1967

WOONSOCKET, RHODE ISLAND

The skies over northern Rhode Island were busy back in 1967. Busy enough that some locals began to carry their cameras around with them, hoping to capture the strange objects they'd seen in the sky. UFOs had been in the region before 1967 and since; however, the sightings reached a peak during this fateful year. There was enough of a flap that busloads of people came to the area from

Boston and other nearby cities to try to see something otherworldly for themselves.

In late June of that year, four girls ages nine to thirteen claimed to have seen an unidentified craft over Wendell Street in the Olneyville section of Providence. Their account made the papers as a tiny curiosity article. But soon, more sightings followed.

A few days later, a story and photo that made the papers concerned Harold A. Trudel of Woonsocket. Trudel was twenty-nine years old, living on Paradis Avenue at the time, and unemployed. He told reporters that on many nights he would grab his World War II–era box camera and drive up to the hills of Woonsocket where he had seen a UFO in the past.

While driving along West Wrentham Road near the Cumberland line, shortly after 5:00 p.m., Trudel spotted a white, domed craft hovering above the trees, so he followed the craft along a dirt road until the saucer was over the power lines. He said the craft was silent and flying about three hundred feet above the ground.

As the craft hovered, Trudel clicked a photograph, and then the UFO sped off out of his view. Around that same time, others in the area reported a rumbling noise, others heard an explosion, and still others saw a fireball in the sky. And then . . . the power went dead.

A spokesperson for Blackstone Valley Electric Company later confirmed that a 23,000-volt transmission line had gone dead in the area where Trudel spotted the UFO. The circuit breakers for the lines never tripped, yet the power failed.

We assume there's a connection between the UFO and the power outage, but it could be a coincidence. Still, Trudel's story and photo made the newspapers and got people buzzing.

Soon, others came forward, and more began watching the skies with their cameras at the ready. Back in 2010, we had the chance to chat with Joe Ferriere at his used-stuff store called "Joe's Moldy Oldies" in Woonsocket. We could describe the store, but we're guessing the name of his business paints a fairly complete picture. Used records, 8-tracks, cassettes, VHS tapes, comic books, used toys you wouldn't let your child play with for fear of what they could catch from them, and Ferriere himself at the helm near the register. Ferriere has since passed away and his store is now long shuttered.

In the mid-1960s, Ferriere saw three craft over the skies of Rhode Island. His experience and those of others prompted him to start his own zine (decades before anyone had ever heard the term *zine*) called *Probe*. Trudel and Ferriere were friends. Trudel had even helped with *Probe* magazine.

Ferriere stated that in June and early July of 1967 he'd been receiving multiple calls each day about a large cylindrical UFO in the area of the Pawtucket Reservoir, so he had to look for himself. On July 3, he set out with camera in hand toward Cumberland.

He pulled into an area west of Diamond Hill Road and walked along the trail beneath the power lines. According to his written account in *Probe* magazine, Ferriere found a clearing about seven hundred to eight hundred feet from the road and began searching for physical evidence of something out of the ordinary. He admitted that he didn't know what he was looking for, and that he could have walked right over something and not known it. Forty-five minutes in, he was about to call off his search when he turned northwest and froze in his tracks.

He said he saw a large, cigar-shaped craft moving silently toward his position. He estimates the craft was 75 to 100 feet in length and flying about 150 to 200 feet above the ground (given that the tallest trees in the area were about 60 feet tall). He described the object as being a drab gray in color, with four circle-shaped lighter spots running along the length of the craft. He also observed a "piston-like apparatus" that slowly moved in and out of one end of the craft. The third distinguishing feature was a trapdoor-like form on the bottom.

Ferriere got to work taking pictures with his camera. Clicking a picture, advancing the film, then sometimes running (and almost falling) to another position to try to take more photos. While watching this silent craft, the hatch opened and he saw a shiny object launched from inside at a high rate of speed—faster than any jet plane, by his estimate. Ferriere clicked more photos of the cigar-shaped craft until it accelerated and passed out of sight over the hill. Then he saw a disk-shaped object that had been ejected from the main craft hovering above the tree line. He also captured a photo of that craft before it quickly accelerated in the same direction as the larger ship.

Ferriere estimates the entire sighting lasted about four minutes. Even when he wrote up his experiences for his magazine, Ferriere refused to speculate as to what (or more accurately *where*) he believed this craft was from.

The more UFO encounters that were published, the more people watched the skies until the sightings eventually died down. What or who these craft were looking for remains a mystery.

Purgatory Chasm's Lover's Leap

MIDDLETOWN, RHODE ISLAND

File this one under: Don't try this! Not at home, and definitely not in Middletown.

Near Sachuest Beach there's a trail that leads to a cliff overlooking the ocean. It's a place called Purgatory Chasm, where they say the Devil once landed after jumping from North Kingstown, Rhode Island, about thirteen miles away. Maybe that mighty landing is what split this cliff rock all those years ago and created a dangerous crack called "Lover's Leap."

An old mid-1800s photo from the Joshua A. Williams's Photograph Rooms studio of Newport features a daguerreotype print of the famous geological feature with the caption "Lover's Leap," so the story has been circulating for more than a century and a half.

At its widest, the fissure is about 12 feet wide. The crack heads inland about 120 feet until it dwindles to nothing where the crack ends. And it's about 40 to 50 feet down to the water below. We'd have to believe that a fall down there could easily be fatal. Which makes jumping across all the more tempting for some. While no one can jump 12 feet, as it moves farther inland, the gap shrinks down to nothing. So there are places where a leap would be easy . . . but what would jumping a one-foot gap prove?

The story of Lover's Leap began in the mid-19th century when Newport was the playground for the very wealthy. The story goes that a beautiful young heiress was making her rounds at all of the fancy summer parties when she caught the eye of a young gentleman who was also in Newport for the summer with his rich family.

It's a tale as old as time, song as old as rhyme. Boy meets girl, and the two are smitten . . . except the young woman decided to play hard to get. The boy was patient, though. They'd flirt at more summer parties, he'd beg the girl for a more proper date, and all the while she was falling for him too.

Weeks went by until finally the young woman agreed to a stroll with her suitor out to the bluffs overlooking the ocean. All through the walk the gentleman professed how happy he thought they could be together. He proclaimed his affection. He made every effort.

When the two reached a mighty crack in the cliffs, the woman told her young suitor to prove his love to her by leaping over the crack and landing safely on the other side. The man looked down, realizing that if he didn't clear the jump it could mean his death. Still, he sighed, took a few steps back . . . then leaped across to land safely on the far side.

The young woman beamed with a smile. That's when her would-be suitor tipped his hat and walked away from her forever. He figured that he might not survive trying to jump through future proverbial hoops for this woman. The crack has been known as "Lover's Leap" ever since.

Rhode Island's Brokenhearted Tower

SOUTH KINGSTOWN, RHODE ISLAND

Just off of Tower Hill Roads in South Kingstown sits a forty-foot observation tower not too far from a rock outcropping. The rock and tower are named after Hannah Robinson, and her story is heartbreaking.

Back in 1770, Hannah Robinson was a beautiful young woman who came from a wealthy family. She was so pretty that men would get tongue-tied around her. They couldn't help themselves. At balls and other social gatherings, potential suitors tried to woo her with poetry and compliments, but Hannah had heard it all before. She found the wealthy men in her life dull and boring. She'd rather play with her spaniel dog, Marcus, than listen to men fall all over themselves to try to talk to her.

But there was one man she didn't find dull and boring: She was enamored of her dance teacher, a young man named Peter Simon. Born in France, Simon came to America to start a new life and find his fortune. He was young, handsome, charming, and a great dancer. Young Hannah was all aflutter when he was around.

Hannah began taking as many dance lessons as she could fit into her schedule. Her mother was also taken by Peter's charm. She convinced her husband to hire Peter to come to their Boston Neck home on Narragansett Bay and offer private instruction to Hannah and her sister.

Pretty soon, love blossomed between Hannah and Peter. However, Hannah's father would never approve of the match

because Peter was poor. So their courtship remained a secret. Hannah would drop love notes out of her window for Peter to retrieve from the bushes below.

This continued for weeks until one day Hannah's father witnessed the note falling into the lilac bushes below Hannah's window. Furious, Mr. Robinson forbade Hannah from ever seeing Peter again.

Hannah was heartbroken, but she was determined to find a way to see her love. A few weeks later, a ball was being thrown at nearby Smith's Castle with Hannah and her sister planning to attend. Hannah's uncle, William Gardiner, also knew of the ball and of Hannah's predicament. William liked Peter Simon very much, and he couldn't stand to see his niece so sad, so William told Peter which night Hannah would be riding through the woods toward Smith Castle.

When Hannah and her sister were en route to the ball, Peter jumped out of the shadows on the road, snatched Hannah from the wagon, and the two lovers rode off to Providence to get married in secret.

Back at Boston Neck, Hannah's father fumed when only one of his daughters returned from the ball that night. He disowned Hannah then and there. He'd already figured out she must have had help, so he demanded to know who had betrayed his wishes. But everyone held their silence.

Back in Providence, Hannah was happy to be with the man she loved. Though her father had disowned her, Peter assured his new bride that this would all blow over and they would be welcomed into the family. But Mr. Robinson was stubborn. He wouldn't hear of it. Weeks turned to months, and soon it became clear that Hannah and Peter were on their own. Though Hannah was in love, being broke wasn't much fun. Plus, she had recently developed a strange cough.

Pretty soon it was clear that Hannah was sick with consumption. Tuberculosis was ravaging parts of New England, and Hannah was just its latest victim. As Hannah grew sicker, Peter discovered that poverty wasn't for him either. He thought he'd married into a wealthy family; instead he had an ailing wife and no fortune. Soon, Peter abandoned his wife, seeking to marry into fortune somewhere else.

When word of Hannah's condition reached Boston Neck, Hannah's father softened. In late October of 1773, Hannah was near death. Mr. Robinson road up to Providence with Hannah's old dog Marcus to keep her company for the ride back home. As the carriage approached the hill that overlooks Boston Neck and Narragansett Bay, Hannah asked her father to stop the carriage so she could sit on a nearby rock and admire the view of her childhood home one last time.

Hannah sat for a while soaking in the view, but soon the autumn air proved too cold for her to bear. Too weak to walk on her own, Hannah's father helped her back to the carriage and back to the Robinson family home. Hannah settled into her bedchamber and breathed her last on October 30. The twenty-seven-year-old woman was gone.

The family told their servants and friends it was the consumption that killed her, but those close to Hannah say she died of a broken heart.

The rock has gone by various names like Crying Rock, Sad Rock, and Meditation Rock, but those who know the story simply call it Hannah's. In 1938, the Civilian Conservation Corps constructed the tower that still sits there today overlooking Hannah's final, brokenhearted view.

Vermont

Born: March 4, 1791

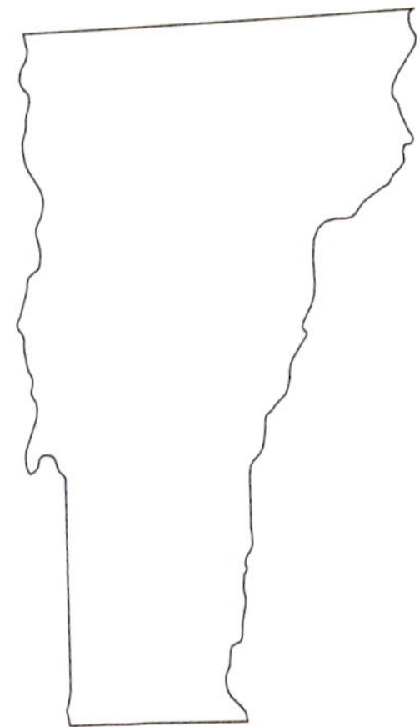

Vermont has always had an independent spirit. From 1777 to 1791, Vermont was its own country, complete with its own military, money, and postal system. Like a child caught in a custody battle between divorcing parents, Vermont sits on land once disputed by both New York and New Hampshire. When asked to choose a side, Vermonters said, "Neither."

Even without recognition from England or the Continental Congress, Vermonters made a go of it for a little while before they figured the rest of the country was going to need their maple syrup, so maybe it was best to get on the same page.

We're thankful they did too, because Vermont has brought us some wonderful weirdness, along with their maple syrup, cheddar cheese, and world-famous ice cream. They've provided us with the strangest burial site in all of New England, a lake monster with dinosaur-like proportions, strange creatures lurking in the mountains, eccentrics we can never forget, and some haunts that still send shivers up our New England spines.

Emily's Haunted Bridge

STOWE, VERMONT

Covered bridges are quintessential old New England. The few remaining examples remind us of bygone eras and simpler times. But one Vermont bridge stands out among all the others because this bridge is haunted.

The Gold Brook Bridge was constructed in 1844. It's fifty feet long, and it's Vermont's only surviving Howe truss–covered bridge. However, few people know it by its official name—most refer to the place as "Emily's Bridge" because her restless spirit roams the old wooden planks.

There are two versions to Emily's legend. In the first, Emily was going to meet her lover one night at the bridge and the two were planning to elope. When he didn't show, she hanged herself from the rafters above. The second version of the story suggests that she was a bride left waiting for her groom at the altar. When he didn't show, she jumped onto her horse and carriage and whipped the horses into top speed as she intended to hunt down her escaping bridegroom. While traveling too fast to negotiate the turn just before the bridge, Emily and the horses tumbled over the edge onto the rocky Gold Brook below and perished.

Though historians are quick to point out that there's no record of any Emily ever dying here, there are a couple of notable accidents at the site. According to the September 15, 1897 *News and Citizen* newspaper in Morrisville, Vermont, "A four horse team from Luce & Lovejoy's stable, driven by Don Smith, and carrying twenty-one passengers was tipped over near Gold Brook Bridge and many occupants injured. A bad place in the road was the cause."

If we jump ahead to 1948, an article in the *Burlington Free Press* reads, "Two Morrisville young men were injured . . . when the car in which they were riding left the Stowe-Waterbury road and landed on its top under the Gold Brook Bridge."

So maybe there's a bit of history mixed with this legend. A warning to travelers. When people enter the bridge—especially late at night—there's talk of hearing the disembodied sounds of a woman weeping. Others have heard phantom footsteps, and they've heard scratching noises on the roofs of their cars, the sound of rope tightening, and even a woman's scream echoing through the rafters. Emily, whoever she was, makes her presence known here at the bridge over Gold Brook.

SPEED LIMIT
NO TRUCKS OR BUSES ALLOWED
BRIDGE WEIGHT LIMIT 4,000 POUNDS

The Curse of Black Agnes

MONTPELIER, VERMONT

Green Mount Cemetery in Montpelier is home to many graves, but none can match the dark reputation of John E. Hubbard's final resting place. The curved stone rail that adorns the back of the monument draws you closer to the weathered-teal-robed bronze statue sitting prominently over Mr. Hubbard's remains . . . but don't get too close . . . this monument might actually kill you. The statue that sits atop Hubbard's final resting place is locally known as Black Agnes.

John Hubbard was a Montpelier businessman who died in 1899 at fifty-three years of age. Though he was known for some of his philanthropic deeds, like building a public library for Montpelier and bequeathing the money to build the Chapel-Vault building on the Green Mount Cemetery grounds, some still accuse him of being a cheapskate and greedy. They claim he could have given more.

Perhaps that's why some believe this grave is cursed. They say that if you sit in the lap of "Black Agnes," you'll be dead within a week. Or horrible luck will follow you. Some claim they believe the statue is that of the Virgin Mary, and no one is supposed to sit on her lap except the baby Jesus.

The bronze statue known as "Black Agnes" was created by Austrian sculptor Karl Bitter. The irony of the name is that this statue isn't even that of a woman. It's a man. It's Death, shrouded, and holding the countenance of someone in extreme anguish.

On either side of the statue are lines from William Cullen Bryant's 1817 poem "Thanatopsis" or "Thoughts on Death."

Thou go not like the
Quarry slave at night
Scourged to his dungeon
But sustained and soothed
By an unfaltering trust.

Approach thy grave
Like one who wraps
The Drapery of his couch
About him and lies down
To pleasant dream.

No matter what gender this statue identifies as, it's creepy and foreboding. But once you know the legend, is sitting on the lap something you'd want to risk?

LIKE ONE WHO
DRAPERY OF
ABOUT HIM AND
TO PLEASANT

File This Under "Strange"

BURLINGTON, VERMONT

When we first saw the thirty-eight-drawer, forty-foot-tall filing cabinet standing proudly yet rusting over the South End of the Burlington skyline, we thought this must be the modern-day cubicle-dweller's totem pole. The Native Americans carved totem poles to tell stories of family lineage, notable events, and village hierarchy. The higher up on the totem pole, the more prestige and clout.

This filing cabinet reminded us of modern-day corporate structure. Each drawer is basically the same as the one below, but still, you'd rather be higher up . . . "Senior Assistant Cubicle Dweller" sounds better than just "Assistant Cubicle Dweller," right?

If you approach the piece, there's no sign offering an explanation, and if you file a complaint in one of the drawers, there's a superb chance that no one will ever see it. Unless you were there when it was placed back in September of 2002, or you made some inquiries, its meaning is left to your own interpretation.

Once we spoke with the sculptor, Bren Alvarez, we learned that we were wrong about the interpretation, but not completely off base. Because this piece offers a commentary on bureaucracy.

Officially called "File Under So. Co., Waiting for . . . ," the filing cabinet tower is a kind of obelisk, and its exact position is no coincidence.

Alvarez, who is both an architect and an artist based in Burlington, was making a comment on the proposed Southern Connector project. This construction project was conceived in 1965 as a way to move traffic from I-89 to downtown Burlington. The point was to ease traffic and make it easy for people to come and go from the city.

Each year the project was discussed, and each year it suffered a series of false starts. At one point, some land was taken by eminent domain that forced multiple families to vacate their homes, but still no road was built. Years came and went, and the discussion continued. At some point one must . . . you know . . . *puff it or pass it*. But not so when talking about large-scale civic projects.

Fast-forward to 2002 and the annual Art Hub display. That's when Alvarez began collecting filing cabinets and building her piece.

"When I was building it, which took a summer, anyone who visited or wandered by would assume that my feelings about the Southern Connector, which is called the Champlain Parkway now, were the same as theirs," Alvarez said. "So everyone interpreted it their own way."

"File Under . . . " has thirty-eight drawers, each drawer representing a year that the Southern Connector had been on the drawing board between 1965 and 2002 (inclusive). Alvarez's next step was to place the piece. "That was a tiny bit sneaky on my part," she said. "It was designed to be part of the annual Art Hub, which is put on by the South End Arts and Business Association. It was

RESIN
Euro Classic

meant to be an outdoor sculpture, which is a category you can participate in."

She called the city engineers to find out where the center line of the proposed Southern Connector would be, and they helped her pick the exact spot for her "temporary" sculpture. And there the piece sat until 2020 when it was moved about a hundred feet across the street. Given how fast the Southern Connector project has been progressing, it's possible we'll all be dead before this sculpture has to move for the actual Champlain Parkway construction project. Clearly, to keep up to date, Alvarez would need to add many more drawers and vertical feet to her sculpture.

The city has come to embrace the sculpture; photos of it have graced their annual report. And at this point, it's become a quirky tourist attraction where people come to honor the gods of bureaucracy, even if they're unaware that those gods still exist and have been in steady control of this non-project since 1965.

Vermont's Sweetest Cemetery

WATERBURY, VERMONT

Just up the hill from the Ben and Jerry's Ice Cream factory in Waterbury sits hallowed ground—a small cemetery, complete with headstones where people can come pay their respects to those who left us far too soon. Headstones like:

TUSKEEGEE CHUNK (1989–1990)
FEATURED PEANUT BUTTER ICE CREAM
WITH CHOCOLATE CHUNKS

The epitaph reads:

LOST FLAVOR SO MELTED. WHO COULD HAVE FORESEEN IT?
PERHAPS WE MISSPELT IT? ADIEU, PRECIOUS PEANUT.

DASTARDLY MASH (1979–1991)
FEATURED CHOCOLATE ICE CREAM WITH PECANS,
ALMONDS, RAISINS, AND CHOCOLATE CHIPS.

The epitaph reads:

HERE THE BRAZEN DASTARDLY LIES.
SOME SAY THAT RAISIN, CAUSED ITS DEMISE.

This is the Ben and Jerry's Flavor Graveyard.

Ben and Jerry's began back in 1978 when two buddies, Ben Cohen and Jerry Greenfield, opened an ice cream shop in a former gas station in Burlington, Vermont. People in Burlington liked their ice cream . . . *a lot*. Pretty soon, the partners couldn't keep up!

Within two years they started packing their ice cream in pints so they could distribute it to grocery stores and other outlets.

The Waterbury factory opened in 1985 and could produce up to 350,000 pints per day. They opened for tours the following year.

Never shy about taking chances with new flavors, Ben and Jerry's tried a lot of different combinations. Some are still around today, others came and went.

In 1997, the Flavor Graveyard was constructed so fans could visit the . . . uhhm . . . dearly de-pinted. Dozens of headstones were erected in the coming years. Then, on October 1, 2015, they took this schtick to the next level by holding an actual funeral for the graveyard's newest tenant: What a Cluster. A hearse pulled up, pall bearers brought out the empty pint container as mourners dressed in black shed their tears.

What a Cluster was peanut butter ice cream with caramel cluster pieces, marshmallow swirls, and peanut butter swirls. The flavor was originally called Clusterfluff . . . but they changed the name in 2011 to the less risqué What a Cluster. A grave was dug, a marker placed with the epitaph:

> GOOEY MARSHMALLOW, CARAMEL AND P.B. WHAT A CLUSTER IT WAS, BUT INEVITABLY. STUFF HAPPENS, SO FOR BETTER OR WORSE, WHAT A CLUSTER WAS TRUCKED AWAY IN THE HEARSE.
> (2011–2014)

Pulling a page from Stephen King's *Pet Sematary*, some of those buried in the Flavor Graveyard don't stay dead . . . if customer demand is high enough, sometimes there are resurrections.

SUGAR PLUM
It swirled in our heads,
It danced in our dreams,
It proved not to be though,
The best of ice creams.
1989-1990
DEVIL'S FOOD CHOCOLATE SORBET
Swirls of Light Chocolate & Dark Chocolate Sorbet
R.I.P.
DEVIL'S FOOD CHOCOLATE
The Devil took the blame
For all the rich indulgence.
now watch him fan the flame,
melting puddles of
wicked succulence.
1996-2001
Aloha Macadamia
2001-2002
Chocolate Chip Cookie Dough Frozen Yogurt
So now we know: our Dough Fro Yo
Just wasn't as great as expected.
Folks who love Dough as well as Fro Yo
Love 'em separate, not interconnected.
1994-2001

The Wampahoofus

MT. MANSFIELD, VERMONT

At 4,393 feet, Mt. Mansfield in northern Vermont is the highest peak in the state. Like many mountains in the region, there are marked hiking trails to guide hikers all the way to the top if they desire. From a distance, Mt. Mansfield looks like a face looking skyward, but to find the mountain's oddest creature, you'll need to get close and climb to at least the 2,600-foot level.

While traversing the Maple Ridge Trail, you may find a sign marking the distance to two other notable locations on the mountain. There's the Forehead, and the famed Wampahoofus Trail. It's around here you should be on the lookout for an odd creature. It's a mammal, they say, that looks like a cross between a deer and a boar. Two of the legs on one side of its body are about half the size of the legs on the other side. Which is why they move so quickly when darting laterally on the steep mountainside. The longer legs reach the lower slope, and the shorter legs are uphill. The males have longer legs on the right and are always moving in a clockwise direction, and the females have longer legs on the left and are always moving counterclockwise. To make more wampahoofuses, they have to intersect just right.

It's believed that the wampahoofus did get the chance to migrate westward—maybe even all the way out to the Great Lakes region because a very clever male and a very clever female figured out that if they lined up their short legs and held them up, they could move on their four long outer legs and get down the mountain.

There are even stories of old Vermont dairy farmers trying to cross-breed their cows with the wampahoofus so the cows could graze better on steep hillsides and mountains.

One theory as to why you won't find one today is that, over time, their legs grew shorter and shorter until they could no longer walk. And it doesn't matter what you call a wampahoofus that can't walk, it ain't coming.

A Bad Case of Taphephobia

NEW HAVEN, VERMONT

Everyone is afraid of death . . . at least a little bit. Death is an ominous wall of doom coming somewhere on the horizon for each and every one of us. To fear death to some extent is natural and normal. However, for people like Timothy Clark Smith, people who suffer from taphephobia, they're not so much afraid of death as they are of being buried alive.

The lengths Smith went through to ensure that he would not be buried prematurely are nothing short of epic.

Timothy Smith was born on June 14, 1821 in Monkton, Vermont. Some highlights from his obituary show a full and colorful life. He graduated from Middlebury College in 1842, then traveled to Washington, DC, where he took a position in the Treasury Department. Next, he studied medicine at the University of New York where he became a medical doctor in 1855. He then left for Russia, where he served as a staff surgeon in the Russian Army during the Crimean War. After the war, he met a woman and fell in love and stayed in Russia for a while before returning to New Haven, Vermont, where he bought the Partch Hotel.

Smith and his wife ran the hotel before he was appointed the consul at Odessa in Russia by President Abraham Lincoln. He remained in Russia for several years before returning to the United States for the education of his older children. He died in New Haven on February 25, 1893, and is now buried in Evergreen Cemetery.

We know for a fact that Smith *must* have been dead at the time of burial because of all the steps he took to ensure that his taphephobia was kept at bay. First, there was his glass-topped coffin. Mourners could look in on him and make sure he wasn't still breathing. Just in case he woke up locked in the casket with no one around, a chisel was placed in one hand, a hammer in the other. Smith could simply knock out the glass and escape.

Then there's his tomb at Evergreen Cemetery. The grave has no marker, but you can't miss it. The cemetery is well-maintained and full of many types of headstones you'd see in just about any boneyard in New England; however, near the street entrance there's a grassy mound with a square of cement at the top. It's the only mound in an otherwise level area.

That square at the top? It's a glass window above a shaft that looks down six feet to where Smith's glass-topped coffin rests below. This unique tomb periodically makes the newspapers because the curious still come by to see it. With the naked eye, you'll see only darkness below. There are some water droplets below the glass, so moisture is getting in. But we could do better than the naked eye. We brought with us a 2,000-lumens flashlight, an iPhone, and a sweatshirt.

The iPhone has a tiny lens that we could lay flat on the glass. The flashlight shined a powerful beam of light below, and the sweatshirt covered the whole thing to block out sunlight from above. This photo offers the best look through the window. As

you can see, moss is growing in through various directions so it's impossible to see to the bottom. However, we like to think that just a little bit of light penetrated down to the bottom where Timothy Clark Smith said, "*Finally* someone is checking on me!"

I Want My Mummy

MIDDLEBURY, VERMONT

West Cemetery in Middlebury offers a vast expanse of headstones and monuments to thousands of people buried here. There are recent burials, and many that go back well over a century. However, hands-down, the oldest person buried here is a child who died back in 1883 . . . that's 1883 *BC*—or almost four thousand years ago if you're keeping score. The child's name is Amun-Her-Khepesh-Ef and he was no less than an Egyptian prince. How he came to rest here—about five thousand miles from home—is an odd tale.

If we jump ahead to 1886 . . . *AD*, the world was gripped with Egypt-fever. Egyptian tombs were being raided, looted, excavated, and dug up in every conceivable way. Museums and private collectors wanted to own a mummy for themselves, so an industry was born.

Henry Sheldon of Middlebury owned and operated the Museum of Vermont History. In 1886, he paid $20 to procure the mummy of a child. Mummies in Egypt were so well-preserved in part because of the dry desert air. But once those mummies were placed on boats and moved through warmer and moister climates, the process of decomposition picked up right where it had left off. By the time the mummy of Amun-Her-Khepesh-Ef arrived in Middlebury, it was in poor shape. The condition was so bad that Sheldon received $10 back. Sheldon figured no one would want to see this partially disintegrated mess, so he placed the remains in a box in the attic of the museum.

After Sheldon died in 1907, the child mummy was forgotten about for decades. That is, until 1945, when a museum employee discovered the mummy in the attic. Allen brought the remains to curator George Mead, but the discovery didn't sit quite right with him. So Mead explained to the museum's board of directors that this had once been a human being, who deserved a proper burial.

The museum board agreed. The Mead family owned a section of West Cemetery, and the curator offered to donate some of his family's burial space. So Amun-Her-Khepesh-Ef's remains were cremated and buried in the Mead family plot. A headstone was placed over the grave that features a Christian cross (though the young Egyptian prince died about two thousand years before the advent of Christianity), the Egyptian ankh, and the outline of a bird, which is the Egyptian hieroglyph representing the soul. The epitaph reads:

ASHES OF AMUN-HER-KHEPESH-EF AGED TWO YEARS
SON OF SENUSRET THE 3RD, KING OF EGYPT
AND HIS WIFE HATHON-HOE-TEP 1883 BC.

Queen Connie and the Beetle

LEICESTER, VERMONT

When you're shopping for a used car, who better to trust than a giant concrete gorilla holding a rusting Volkswagen Beetle? At least that's what its creator hoped you would think.

When driving down Route 7 in Leicester, you can't miss the giant gorilla named Queen Connie. Erected in 1987, she's the work of sculptor T. J. Neil. Neil pitched the idea to the owner of Pioneer Auto Sales as a roadside oddity that would command international attention. At first Neil suggested a giant pioneer figure to go with the name of the business, but that was nixed in favor of a giant gorilla—something King Kong–like. However, the business owner, Joan O'Neil-Gittens, insisted that the gorilla be female in honor of the first female car salesperson and dealership owner in Vermont. So female it was. The auto dealer sponsored a contest for local schoolchildren to name her, and "Queen Connie" was the winner, earning the kid who thought of it a brand-new red bicycle.

Queen Connie still stands where she's been since 1987, and Her Royal Weirdness is still proudly holding up that old VW Bug. The sculpture has even outlived the sculptor, who passed away in 2010.

The Phineas Gage Incident

CAVENDISH, VERMONT

Today, on a stone in Cavendish, there's a monument to a medical miracle. Back in 1848, a railroad construction mishap led to an event that has had medical professionals eternally scratching their heads as to how Phineas Gage survived his infamous accident.

On September 13, 1848, at around 4:30 in the afternoon, twenty-five-year-old railroad worker Phineas Gage was setting some explosives in some rocks to help clear the way for the Rutland and Burlington Railroad. A hole had been bored into the rock, and Gage was filling that hole with black blasting powder. Next, he lifted his three-and-a-half-foot-long, one-and-one-quarter-inch-diameter, thirteen-pound tamping bar and began to tamp down the black powder for maximum effectiveness when they set the charge. While tamping down the powder, the metal bar inadvertently sparked the powder, setting off an explosion that launched the tamping bar out of the blasting hole like a missile and right through Gage's left cheek and up through the top of his skull.

Gage was knocked to the ground. When the other workers saw the bar lodged through his face and skull, they knew he was dead . . . except he lay there twitching and shaking. The other men watched in horror as Gage began to pull at the tamping bar, sliding it out from within his skull. With the bar out, and Gage bleeding profusely, the others were sure he would die in moments . . . but he didn't.

Gage was brought back to his hotel where he sat in a chair awaiting the doctor. Physician Edward H. Williams would later recount the scene in a medical journal. Williams wrote:

> When I drove up he said, "Doctor, here is business enough for you." I first noticed the wound upon the head before I alighted from my carriage, the pulsations of the brain being very distinct. The top of the head appeared somewhat like an inverted funnel, as if some wedge-shaped body had passed from below upward. Mr. Gage, during the time I was examining this wound, was relating the manner in which he was injured to the bystanders. I did not believe Mr. Gage's statement at that time, but thought he was deceived. Mr. Gage persisted in saying that the bar went through his head. Mr. Gage got up and vomited; the effort of vomiting pressed out about half a teacupful of the brain [through the exit hole at the top of the skull], which fell upon the floor.

After surgeries to stop the bleeding and patch his wounds, Gage continued to dumbfound the doctors by surviving and healing. He lost an eye due to infection, but could still walk and talk a few weeks later.

Gage was studied a year after his accident and researchers found that his personality had changed. He claimed he felt "off" at times. After becoming famous in the medical journals, Gage moved to San Francisco to be with his parents. He became prone to epileptic seizures and convulsions, and eventually died in 1860 at the age of thirty-six. He survived eleven years after an incident that *should* have killed him.

Champ the Lake Monster

LAKE CHAMPLAIN, VERMONT

The Loch Ness Monster in Scotland is the most famous lake monster in the world, but New England's version may run a close second at this point. For centuries, people have talked and written about a serpent-like monster lurking in the waters of Lake Champlain.

Lake Champlain is huge. It shares the Vermont and New York borders to the lake's east and west, and its northern tip resides in Quebec. It's 120 miles long and 12 miles at its widest point, it has an average depth of 64 feet, and the lake is 400 feet at its deepest point. The lake features 435 square miles of surface water.

If we go back over half a millennium to the time when the Abenaki and Iroquois people lived in this region, we find the earliest accounts of a strange creature in these waters. They called it *Tatoskok*, which roughly translates to "great serpent." It was described as an underwater horned serpent that was known to eat humans.

In July of 1609, French explorer Samuel de Champlain saw this lake and knew because of its size and location that it would be an important resource for commercial shipping. And that also meant it was of significant military importance. The lake would eventually be named in Champlain's honor.

The story goes that Champlain had heard about the monster back then too, maybe even had a sighting of his own. But monster

or not, this body of water was too important to be concerned about everything that lurks in its waters.

As more colonists established farms, then towns, and even cities around the lake, the stories and eyewitness accounts piled up in the local lore and eventually in the newspapers.

The descriptions of Champ vary only slightly. A serpent about one hundred feet long with a head like a horse. They called it a "serpent" for many decades. But then "serpent" wasn't enough. It became a monster. In 1887, this creature even caught the attention of circus magnate P. T. Barnum, who offered a $50,000 reward for anyone who could catch this beast dead or alive.

By the 1940s and 1950s, Champ the Lake Monster was becoming a cottage industry. People speculated as to what Champ could be. Some not-yet-documented creature? A dinosaur left over from another era?

Though the dinosaur theory may sound strange, consider that there's an island on this lake called Isle La Motte on the Vermont side that's home to the oldest known fossil reef in the world. It dates back over 450 million years.

New England also has a long history of giant serpents fitting Champ's description, but those animals have been found near the shores of our ocean, not in a freshwater lake.

One man who will never forget what he saw on Lake Champlain is Steven Mazuroski. In July of 1978, he and his father were at their family's campground on the lake overlooking the water. Mazuroski, who grew up on the lake, said:

> The camp itself is up on a rise. We have a good view of the lake and it was where the lake was like glass. It was very calm. My father looked over and he said, "Hey, look at that!" And I looked out and just outside the bay where the camp is, there

was something in the water traveling north. It had a very long and thin wake, which was important to me because it was something going through the water instead of on top of the water. The description of it would be like a horse's head without ears. My father and I were watching it and it was traveling quite rapidly. It came up a little bit and my dad said, "Look! There's a neck!" At that time there was a boat coming south and when they got a little close, the head went underwater and never reappeared. The boat went by and apparently they saw nothing. My dad looked at me and said, "Ah! We've just seen the Lake Champlain Monster!"

Mazuroski said that, when he was young, he heard the old-timers refer to it as "Old Blue."

Boats armed with sonar have looked for Champ, there have been multiple expeditions trying to prove that he's real, but so far Champ remains elusive.

Hundreds of witnesses have come forward in more modern times. Today, Champ is an industry unto himself. There are statues of him around the lake, plush toys and T-shirts for sale, and, in Burlington, they have a professional baseball team that's the farm team for the Oakland A's. Their mascot is, of course, Champ the Lake Monster.

Believe in him or don't, he's omnipresent around this lake to the point where even if you're the most hardened skeptic, you can't walk by Lake Champlain without gazing out on the water and wondering if you might be the next person to see a monster.

The Curse of the Cemetery Vine

EAST DUMMERSTON, VERMONT

Dummerston Center Cemetery is the permanent home of over eight hundred people. Headstones date back as far as the mid-1700s and, like countless small-town boneyards, there are various local families buried in different sections of the land. For most people, death is a surprise, taking our loved ones without giving us advance notice. But the Spaulding family in Dummerston claim that there was a sinister subterranean sign as to when the next family member would fall.

When you walk along the neat row of Spaulding graves, you'll see how young many of them were when they died: Mary Spaulding Laughton, 1761–1782 (age twenty); Esther Spaulding, 1768–1783 (age fourteen); Timothy Spaulding, 1765–1785 (age twenty); Leonard Spaulding Jr., 1760–1792 (age thirty-two; Reuban Spaulding, 1756–1794 (age thirty-eight); and Josiah Spaulding, 1770–1798 (age twenty-eight). Most of them died from tuberculosis.

It was Josiah Spaulding's death that unraveled a preternatural curse some claim was plaguing this family. Back in November of 1798, Josiah Spaulding succumbed to tuberculosis. His mother, Margaret, who lived with Josiah and his wife, was beside herself with grief. She had already lost so many children to tuberculosis, and she'd lost her husband in 1788, though he was buried east of the hollow because the cemetery grounds were

Josiah Spaulding
year

soaked with water at the time he died. She believed her family was cursed.

Back then, tuberculosis was more commonly called "consumption" because it consumed its victims from the inside out. Why it decimated some families and communities and not others sometimes came down to a matter of belief. Those who were spared may feel that God protected them. Those who lost most of their families believed that they were the victims of a curse or a vampire. The only way to know for certain was to exhume the dead.

At the Dummerston Cemetery, Margaret convinced her family that they needed to dig up the most recently deceased to look for signs of vampirism. Bodies had to be examined to look for proper decay, or telltale signs, like the corpse had moved or was not decomposed because it was feeding on the living. The Spauldings weren't the first nor the last to attempt this superstitious and creepy practice.

When they dug down to the most recent burial, they found that a curious black tree root had engulfed the coffin. This was strange because there were no nearby trees. They followed the black root to the next most recent Spaulding burial and found a similar sight. Margaret insisted that the entire root must be removed and destroyed. The work took almost the entire day to complete. And then as a finale, she had a surgeon open her son Josiah's chest cavity, remove his vital organs, and had them burned in a fire just to be certain that the vampire's spell was broken.

They say the curse was lifted that day because the next Spaulding to die made it to more than four decades later. The Spaulding headstones are all still there, but, thankfully, the cursed black root is long gone.

The Buff Ledge Camp UFO Abduction

COLCHESTER, VERMONT

Near the shores of Lake Champlain sits the former Buff Ledge Summer Camp in Colchester. For the better part of the 20th century, this was a place for young girls to experience lakeside summers and all that nature has to offer. But back in 1968, this camp was the setting for an alleged out-of-this-world UFO abduction that still brings out alien-hunting pilgrims today.

Before rebranding itself as Buff Ledge in the 1950s, the camp was called Norfleet, and before that this was the site of Camp Champlain. The camp remained in operation until 1980, when it shut down for good. But an event that took place on August 7, 1968, left a permanent mark on the psyches of two witnesses, and on the region forever.

In the summer of 1968, sixteen-year-old Michael Lapp worked as a camp counselor at Buff Ledge. On the evening of August 7, Lapp and Janet Cornell, a nineteen-year-old counselor, were on the docks watching the sunset when they saw a "glowing, cigar-shaped object" in the sky. Soon, three smaller objects emerged from the larger object.

When the craft approached closer to the dock, Lapp claimed that he saw two figures appear through the dome above the vehicle. Lapp said these creatures communicated telepathically with him. The message was that they were not here to hurt him; they had come to Earth to gather "some kind of energy."

Lapp then said the craft fired a beam of light at him and his fellow counselor before they lost consciousness. They woke up when they heard the voices of the campers returning from their swim meet. The UFO then fired off several flashes of light before it faded out of sight.

The story sat dormant for years until Lapp contacted author and UFO researcher Walter Webb. Webb interviewed the witnesses and observed hypnotic regressions with each. He concluded in his 1994 book, *Encounter at Buff Ledge*, that the two were telling the truth.

Whether that UFO was also here to see if they could spot Champ, the lake monster of Lake Champlain, will forever remain a mystery.

Who's Buried in Ethan Allen's Tomb?

BURLINGTON, VERMONT

If you stroll the grounds of Green Mount Cemetery in Burlington, you can't miss the forty-two-foot-tall monument to the city's most notable figure: Revolutionary War hero Major General Ethan Allen, the founder of Vermont, and the guy with a furniture company named after him.

The only problem is . . . *Ethan Allen's body isn't there*. And *no*, we don't know where it is anymore.

Ethan Allen moved his family to Burlington in 1789. At fifty-two, he'd already led a colorful life and was considered a hero

by his neighbors. A theologian, scholar, businessman, and farmer, Allen did it all.

Those who knew him considered Allen at times crude and rude. But a book he published in 1785 earned him the most enemies. The book was titled *Reason, the Only Oracle of Man*. *Reason* was an attack on Christianity and the Bible. Allen had a real problem with the power of established churches and especially priests. The solution, Allen proposed, was more of a deistic approach, where man is a free agent in the natural world.

The book was a flop in all senses—a critical flop and a financial flop. It sold only two hundred copies. Of course, most of his critics were clergy, who were the very target of Allen's attacks, but still, in the late 1700s, clergy held a lot of sway. Allen *was* a hero, but he'd made some enemies along the way as well.

In February of 1789, Allen and an employee made a twenty-five-mile journey to pick up a load of hay. The following morning on the ride back home, Allen wasn't feeling well. His body convulsed, and then he slumped over, unconscious. With no other options, his driver knew the only hope was to return to Burlington as quickly as possible.

The driver did get him back home, but Allen passed away a few hours later.

On February 16, Ethan Allen was given a funeral filled with all of the pomp and circumstance befitting a war hero and a state founder. Though some of the newspapers extolled the patriot as a great man who served the public, his clergy critics had not forgotten what he'd written about them and were quick to offer a sentiment of *good riddance*.

After the public said its goodbyes, the family held a private burial at Green Mount Cemetery. The headstone epitaph read:

The corporeal part of General Ethan Allen
rests beneath this stone. The 12th day of February 1789.
Aged 51 years. His spirit tried the mercies of his God
in whom he alone believed and strongly trusted.

It's worth noting that Allen was fifty-two.

By 1851, besides a lot more burials in Green Mount Cemetery, not a lot had changed, except that Ethan Allen's headstone was now missing. It had been stolen.

In 1852, the Vermont Legislature authorized the construction of a grand monument made from Vermont granite. The stone at the base reads:

Vermont to Ethan Allen.
Born in Litchfield, Connecticut, 10th January AD 1737.
Died in Burlington, Vermont, 12th February AD 1789
and buried near the site of this monument

You may be thinking, *Okay, fair enough, the monument is close to where his original grave was located*. However, when the ground was excavated to lay the foundation for the monument, they dug exactly where his grave was supposed to be because they wanted his mortal remains under the giant column. They had the cemetery plot map from sixty-nine years earlier. They knew where to dig. The only problem was they found nothing. No tomb. No casket. No body. Nothing.

The plot thickened when a letter was written to the local newspaper from a man in Kalamazoo, Michigan, who claimed his wife's aunt was Ayres B. Allen, the widow of Captain Hannibal Allen, General Ethan Allen's eldest son. The aunt claimed Ethan Allen was buried in Bennington, Vermont, not Burlington. Not only is that a dubious and distant connection at best, but there's also no record of it.

Was the body of Vermont's founder and one of their most notable and favorite sons lost, stolen, or never buried in the first place?

The phrase "buried near the site of this monument" could be relative, we guess.

An Ice Age Monster from the Deep

BRANDON, VERMONT

We know from fossil records that giant beasts once walked among us. We flippantly say the dinosaurs are extinct now, there's nothing to worry about, but most of us know that's just not true. Birds are all descendants of the dinosaur. And then there are other creatures, like alligators and crocodiles that, while not technically dinosaurs, have been around for 200 million years and clearly have "the look." And what about Ice Age monsters? Could they still be frozen somewhere ready to come back and terrorize us?

A curious news article about an event in Brandon, Vermont, makes us wonder.

Brandon was once home to the Forest Dale Ironworks. The ironworks began in 1810, using ore mined locally. In 1823, a blast furnace was installed to produce pig iron and then later the facility was used to produce parlor stoves.

In July of 1865, America was beginning its long recovery from the Civil War. The nation needed tools and iron to rebuild, so workers in Brandon dug. In addition to the iron mine, Brandon was home to an ochre mine. The ochre was ground into powder to be used as an adhesive resin for mounting tools onto handles.

One hot July day, workers were digging around the 110-foot level of the mine when a shovel sank into a muddy pocket. There was great concern because if this shovel broke into an underground vein of water, the tunnel could flood in minutes, dooming everyone stuck inside. Thankfully, it was just mud, but from the mud came some kind of creature over a foot in length. After wiping away some dirt, the workers saw the largest frog they'd ever seen. They figured it was some Ice Age relic frozen underground and preserved. So they brought it to the surface.

After rinsing it off, the frog measured fourteen inches from its nose to its butt. With extended legs, it would be over two-and-a-half feet in length. Local kids came to check out the odd find, and that's when the strange find got even stranger. According to a 1922 article in the *Brattleboro Reformer* newspaper, the frog began to convulse, twitch, and then leap back to life. Some workers put the frog in a sack and carried it to a nearby pond.

In North America, the largest bullfrogs can grow to six to eight inches in length—that's from the tip of the nose to the butt. And weigh two to three pounds. If we're to believe the newspaper, this Vermont frog was twice that size.

Frank Rogers of Brandon was quoted in the article, claiming he was there as a kid and witnessed the giant frog after they pulled it from the ground. He also said they could hear that frog for several summers after. Its "ribbit" echoed throughout the region.

Vermont's Haunted Police Academy

PITTSFORD, VERMONT

Police work is difficult. The training can be grueling. You're meant to be tested physically and mentally to ensure that you're cut out for the job. So imagine doing your police training in a haunted building. That's what's expected of Vermont police officers.

Cadets sleeping in the dorm rooms have experienced strange activity, such as hearing footsteps and lights switching on or off by themselves. But most concerning is seeing a ghostly woman checking on them in their rooms.

Today the Police Academy in Pittsford looks stately, almost like a college campus; however, this complex wasn't always a police training facility. It used to be a hospital for tuberculosis patients. For many decades, tuberculosis ravaged the local communities.

Built in 1907 as a tuberculosis sanatorium, this Pittsford facility only took in patients with mild cases of the illness. Part of the point of sanatoriums like this one was to keep the infected away from others to help stop the spread.

By 1918, Vermont—and, frankly, a large portion of the world—had a very big problem. World War I had been raging for years. Countless soldiers were thrown into difficult conditions and tight quarters. Tuberculosis had a chance to spread far and wide, thanks to the Great War. As soldiers returned home from overseas, many of them had contracted the illness, so the Vermont sanatorium erected tents and other temporary structures to accommodate the influx of sick patients.

Caring for the sick is a selfless and dangerous act. The staff, doctors, and nurses were always careful, but sometimes the caregivers became patients. That was the story with nurse Mary. She was always considered attentive, kind, and a ray of sunshine until she too took ill and then died from the illness she'd been fighting in so many others.

The Pittsford Sanatorium for Tuberculosis closed in 1970, but the grounds weren't empty for long. The facility was converted into the Vermont Police Academy, which is what it's been ever since. Though the purpose of the facility is now quite different than before, some echoes and shades of the past are still reported here.

By the firing range, especially on foggy days, sometimes instructors and cadets will claim they see a woman in a white nurse's tunic drift by the gun range. And inside the dormitories, a ghostly nurse has been known to check on the rooms of her former patients. The police cadets don't feel alarmed—they believe she's a warm and caring presence. But no matter who you are, it's always unnerving to experience a visitor in the dead of night and to know there's no one you can call to haul this intruder away.

A Haunted Tower in the Woods

BRATTLEBORO, VERMONT

As you approach through the forest, the Retreat Tower looks like a lone medieval castle spire perched on a hilltop. Though there were no knights or shining armor, this place was a refuge for some, and the end of the line for at least one other.

Old asylums are universally creepy. Maybe that's because it doesn't take much for our minds to wander to a place where we see that we're just one hardship too many away from ending up in a facility like the hospital in Brattleboro.

The Brattleboro Retreat Center was born from the death of Anna Hunt Marsh in 1834, who bequeathed $10,000 for the construction of the Vermont Asylum for the Insane. Based on the Quaker concept of moral treatment, this new facility was a bold departure from how the mentally ill were usually cared for.

The facility opened in 1836, with forty-eight patients residing at the asylum. By the mid-1880s, the population had swelled to 450 patients. To mark fifty years of service to its patients, Superintendent Dr. Joseph Draper lobbied his board for construction of a castle-like spire that would overlook the hospital campus and the surrounding community.

Construction began in 1887, with many patients helping with the building project. Materials were procured from local quarries, and brick by brick this castle-like spire rose from the ground until the work suddenly stopped. With funds running low, the project

was left unfinished. For five years, the castle spire sat half-done until the death of Dr. Draper. His colleagues realized that the best way to honor their beloved superintendent was to finish his building project.

Once completed, the castle tower was sixty-five feet tall, complete with five-hundred-pound granite blocks forming the quoins of the castle turret. The view from the top is breathtaking. You can see downtown Brattleboro to the southeast, the Connecticut River to the east, and the hospital grounds near the river.

With such a high spire so close to where the mentally ill were being treated, one would think this place would lend itself to tragic suicides. However, in searching the history here, we find only one: In June of 1923, Metropolitan Opera House cellist Carl Dodge was being treated at the hospital for a nervous breakdown. His body was discovered at the base of this tower . . . but Dodge didn't jump. A revolver was found near his hand.

Today, this castle spire sits where it has for more than a century. Surrounded by hiking trails in the woods, the tower suddenly rises above you. You hear the stories of patient suicide, you see this isolated structure, and realize that the haunted reputation does not take much imagination. Whether visitors tune in to the despair of former patients, or if the high tower allows our minds to go to a dark place, if only for a second, the Brattleboro Retreat Tower conjures up emotions and connections to those who came here during the most troubling periods of their lives. Those hands were placed on each of these bricks, and we realize: There but for the grace of God, go we.

Little Maggie: Newport's Fisherwoman

NEWPORT, VERMONT

Eccentrics stick out. If there's a photo to prove it—all the better! That was the case of Little Maggie who was once considered the most photographed person around Lake Memphremagog in northern Vermont. She was a vagabond who wore men's clothes, loved to fish, loved to smoke, and loved to get her picture taken. She was a roamer and adventurer, always moving all of her ninety-one years.

Maggie Little was born in Bolton, Quebec. As a kid she was always wandering off in the woods alone and exploring the world

SKIDOO! 23

around her. When she was twelve, her family moved thirty miles south to East Berkshire, Vermont.

After arriving in East Berkshire, Maggie couldn't get herself settled. Each day she'd wander farther and farther from home until one day she just kept walking.

The world can be a dangerous place for a young girl out there completely on her own, but Maggie's secret weapon was her kindness. At barely five feet tall, she was shorter than most, which is why folks took to calling Maggie Little "Little Maggie."

She made friends everywhere she went, and she was *not* looking for handouts. She was willing to work, whether that meant chopping wood or doing other chores faster and better than men much older and bigger than she was. She'd work for some money, or room and board for a few days, but never too long because she liked to keep moving.

Her favorite way to feed herself was by fishing. She spent many hours fishing the shores of Lake Memphremagog. She always wore a conservative dress over her legs, but often paired it with a man's coat and hat. Her pipe was never far from her lips, leaving rings of smoke wherever she roamed.

When she ran low on tobacco or money, she'd find another odd job to replenish her supply and return to her vagabond ways.

In Little Maggie's later years, her mother had moved to Newport, Vermont, so Maggie found herself in town visiting quite a bit. By the turn of the 20th century, Lake Memphremagog was turning into quite the tourist destination. Visitors came with their cameras and would ask to take pictures of Little Maggie because she looked like no one else.

That's when an idea struck her: If you wanted to take her picture, you needed to offer her a few coins or fill her pipe for her. And tourists did.

By 1930, Maggie was in her late eighties and too weak to work. She moved into the poor farm, but still came to Newport to chat with locals and visitors and continued to get her photo taken right up until the end.

The last paragraph of her obituary in the February 12, 1934 *St. Johnsbury Republican* newspaper reads: "Little Maggie has gone on one more adventure, her last one, and one wonders if she will be content to stay put when she has been led through the pearly gates, or if after a while she will still hanker to wander somewhere else."

The Bellows Falls Petroglyphs

BELLOWS FALLS, VERMONT

Off the banks of the Connecticut River, just below the Vilas Bridge in the town of Bellows Falls, some petroglyphs stare out at you like ancient emojis from a lost time.

Carved into the rock face are some round and oblong, but basic, faces. Some are just two dots for eyes and a line for a mouth, and a few of them have what appear to be antennae jutting out from the tops of their heads.

During the summer of 1789, word of these strange markings reached the ear of Reverend David McClure of Dartmouth College. McClure came to Bellows Falls to study the rocks. He'd never seen anything like these petroglyphs before. If the Abenaki

people made a habit of creating these kinds of carvings, he would expect to find them all over the region. But he didn't. He believed the carvings dated back to between three hundred and three thousand years earlier.

When Bellows Falls was founded and first settled in the 1750s, town founders made note of the carvings. Some speculated that this section of the river offered good fishing, so maybe this was some kind of marking to tell others this was a good spot. Others suspected this must have been a sacred site for the Abenaki.

Reverend McClure interpreted the lines extending off the tops of some of the heads as devil horns; maybe this was an evil place full of demons. More likely, McClure was allowing his own religious and ethnic bias to cloud his interpretation.

In 1857, ethnologist Henry Schoolcraft studied the petroglyphs and believed maybe they depicted a battle scene. A year later, historian Benjamin Hall wrote that maybe the group of faces might have represented a chief and his tribe. In more recent times, coauthors William Haviland and Marjory Power, who wrote the book *The Original Vermonters,* studied the Bellows Falls petroglyphs. They believe this location was a sacred place for the Abenaki, that shamans came here to enter a trance-like state and see visions. Perhaps they carved those visions on the rocks in front of them.

Though McClure only described three faces in his initial study, it's believed that there were as many as twenty-four at one point, but some had faded due to time and natural erosion, so it's difficult to be sure. In the 1930s, the Daughters of the American Revolution hired a stone mason to come here and deepen the existing glyphs to preserve them. Sadly, this means that what we're seeing today isn't exactly what was left here long ago.

In reality, we'll never get a definitive answer as to who carved these faces and why, meaning the petroglyphs and the mystery will endure. . . . Depending on which television programs you watch, maybe this is ancient graffiti, or maybe . . . it's aliens! *We're* not saying it's aliens, but we can't stop *you* from saying it.

Maine

Born: March 15, 1820

Eastport, Maine, is the easternmost city in the United States, meaning folks in Eastport see the sunrise before the rest of us. Considering that Maine already gets a jump on the day (and because, out of the six New England states, chronologically, they were the last to join the Union), Maine will bat last in our lineup of Northeastern weirdness.

Maine's got water: almost 3,500 miles of coastline, and over 4,000 islands, plus 32,000 miles of rivers and streams. The ocean has always provided for the people who live there.

Maine is known for its lobster and seafood (we once ate lobster-flavored ice cream at a shop in Bar Harbor). They take their seafood seriously too! On January 26, 1939, Maine Representative Cleveland Sleeper Jr. introduced a bill titled, "A Bill to Prohibit the Use of Tomatoes as an Ingredient in the Preparation of Maine Clam Chowder." The penalty for the offender? Digging a barrel of clams at high tide. Thankfully, the bill passed, and balance was restored in the universe (with the exception of Manhattan, New York, and that abomination they call clam chowder).

Maine gave us the donut, a soda called Moxie that started a war that rages to this day, sea monsters, strange tales of beasts from their vast wilderness, hauntings, hermits, and the tall tale of the most famous lumberjack of all time.

The Haunting of Portland Head Lighthouse

CAPE ELIZABETH, MAINE

Maine's oldest lighthouse is also among its most haunted.

Construction of the Portland Head Light began in 1787 by directive of George Washington. Built from local stone and materials, the original tower stood fifty-eight feet tall. But when the masons completed the initial task, they realized the light wouldn't be visible to the south, so the tower was raised another twenty feet.

Fueled by whale oil lamps, Portland Head Light entered service on January 10, 1791. The job of the keeper is lonely and mundane, but also critical to the safety of countless ships and sailors. Yet no matter how well you tend to your duties, accidents happen, and sometimes the sea and nature combine to become a foe that even the brightest light can't overcome.

Throughout the storied history of Portland Head Light, there have been tragedies. Painted on a rock next to the lighthouse are the words, *ANNIE C. MAGUIRE* SHIPWRECKED HERE CHRISTMAS EVE 1886. The ship was bound for Portland Harbor from Buenos Aires. Lighthouse keeper Joseph Strout recalled the night to be snowy with low visibility, which may explain why the ship ran aground. Fortunately, all aboard were brought to the safety of the keeper's quarters where they had food and shelter until they could be transported to Portland.

Though all were rescued from the *Maguire*, other ships weren't as fortunate. In 1864, the *Bohemian* from Liverpool was wrecked near the lighthouse point, resulting in the deaths of forty of its immigrant passengers. Some claim you can still hear their cries for help coming from near the rocks. Those cries haunt lighthouse keepers. It's a reminder of the magnitude of the job.

Joseph Strout was the longest-serving lighthouse keeper, from 1869 to 1904. Though he's been relieved by other lighthouse keepers, and now the automation of the light thanks to the US Coast Guard, his spirit may still be here keeping watch, still tending to his duties.

Poet and Portland native Henry Wadsworth Longfellow grew up around this lighthouse. The young scribe recognized the immortality of this place—both the people and the beacon. Many believe growing up in the shadow of Portland Head Light is what inspired his poem "The Lighthouse."

Steadfast, serene, immovable, the same,
Year after year, through all the silent night
Burns on forevermore that quenchless flame,
Shines on that inextinguishable light!

The Big Birth of Paul Bunyan

BANGOR, MAINE

Paul Bunyan is the most famous lumberjack in the nation. They say he could create a lake by stomping his foot. They say his camp stove was an acre in size and his hotcake griddle was greased by men wearing sides of bacon for skates. They say he could fell a forest with one swipe of his mighty axe. He, along with his giant blue ox named Babe, were fixtures anywhere lumberjacks have plied their trade. If you ask folks around Maine where he's from originally, they'll tell you Bangor.

Sure, other states like Wisconsin, Michigan, and Minnesota may stake their claim to the giant's birthplace, but in Bangor, there's a thirty-one-foot-tall statue of Bunyan on Main Street, and City Hall proudly displays his framed birth certificate, claiming that Bunyan entered the world via Maine on February 12, 1834. (It's worth noting that the birth certificate was dated and signed January 29, 1959.)

Back in the 1850s, Bangor was a huge lumber port. Maine's vast forests fed the mills and ships that hauled away the timber to help build America. Being a lumberjack was grueling work, and often dangerous. Lumberjacks were competitive with each other: Who has the fastest axe? Who can drop the most trees in a day? And so on. Legends were born of lumberjacks bigger, stronger, and better than all the others. Paul Bunyan became the subject of a folktale worthy of aspiration.

The statue of Bunyan was unveiled in Bangor on February 12, 1959, on what would have been Paul's 125th birthday, according to his birth certificate signed two weeks earlier—almost as if some town official knew this $20,000, thirty-one-foot-tall, 3,700-pound statue was coming to town.

A Witch's Curse on Colonel Buck's Grave

BUCKSPORT, MAINE

There's a monument in the cemetery of Bucksport that many say is cursed by a witch. And the proof of that curse is obvious to anyone who offers the slightest glance at the obelisk bearing town founder Jonathan Buck's last name. The brown, rusted outline of a leg with a pointy toe can be seen on the front. Locals will tell you it's the leg of a witch that Jonathan Buck condemned to death.

In June of 1763, Colonel Buck settled the area known as Plantation No. 1, opened its first sawmill, and helped establish the town. The area was growing and life was good, but there was trouble brewing in the form of the Revolutionary War. The British had just built Fort George at the mouth of Penobscot Bay, meaning they controlled the traffic heading up and down the river. On April 17, 1779, Colonel Buck took up arms, along with most of the men from the plantation, and led the Penobscot Expedition effort to burn Fort George to the ground. The effort was valiant, but also a disaster. Buck and his men failed to stop the British and, worse, the day following the attack, the British sailed into the defenseless Plantation No. 1 and burned the buildings of anyone who didn't swear allegiance to the Crown.

By the time the Revolutionary War ended in 1783, Jonathan Buck returned to Plantation No. 1 to rebuild, and the town was named Buckstown Plantation in his honor.

In the early 1790s, Buck was a leader of the town named after him, and he intended to make his namesake dignified in every way, so when accusations that witchcraft was afoot in their community, Buck acted quickly. The legend goes that he ordered an old hag of a woman to be burned at the stake.

As the pyre was being set around the old witch, she stared Buck in the eyes and announced for all to hear, "I will dance on your grave!"

Jonathan Buck died on March 18, 1795, and was buried in the cemetery in town. This proud obelisk was erected a few feet away from his actual grave and headstone by his descendants in August of 1852 because they felt the town, now called Bucksport, needed a more substantial memorial to its founder. Soon after, a strange stain formed on the front of the stone bearing the distinct outline of a pointy toe and a lower leg.

Though there's no record of a witch execution in town, the dancing leg is unmistakable, and has haunted Buck's memorial for over 150 years.

Bill Knights's Ghost Haunts Rufie Brown

WEST ATHENS, MAINE

On April 21, 1905, after a night of drinking hard cider with Rufus Brown Jr. and his fourteen-year-old wife, fifty-nine-year-old Bill Knights wound up dead. Though Knights lived in Bingham, he spent most of his time in what was called the Brown-Tuttle settlement in West Athens. Brown-Tuttle was practically a shantytown in the woods occupied by members of the two families. When the logging jobs moved away, the economy dried up, leaving this collection of homes and shacks to fend for themselves.

"Rufie," as he was known by his friends, thought Knights was paying too much attention to Rufie's young wife. Rufie threatened Knights, then stormed off to fetch a shotgun from his father-in-law next door. With loaded gun in hand, Rufie yelled for Knights to come out of the house. When Knights refused, Rufie shot the gun at his own house, hitting the roof. When Knights finally emerged to try to defuse the situation, Rufie hit him in the head with the butt of his shotgun and killed him instantly. Other witnesses claim Rufie hit him in the head with the gun two or three more times for good measure.

When the sheriff arrived and took Rufie to jail, no one seemed to care. "The affair is considered by the whole neighborhood as a good joke," the April 22, 1905 *Daily Kennebec Journal* account said, "and it appears to be a matter of entire indifference to both 'Rufie' and his parents whether he passes the rest of his days in Thomaston [prison] or not."

By August, Rufie Brown was in the news again for being haunted by the ghost of Bill Knights. Those who live there claimed the community was haunted since the day of the murder. The article reads, "John and 'Mitt' Avery, whose house Bill usually made his headquarters, solemnly aver that Bill has been there since the murder—once actually dragging the bed-clothes off them at night. Rufie Brown, Jr., who is charged with killing Knights, says he sees 'Ole Bill most every night, but said, 'Damn him, I hain't 'fraid of 'im.'"

Bill Knight's Ghost Haunts Rufie Brown.

West Athens Residents Terrorized by Strange Nightly Visitations Since Knight's Murder—Bill's "Ghost" Tears Bedclothes.

America's Last Crank Call

WOODSTOCK, MAINE

Those of us old enough to remember the days before every phone featured caller ID may recall crank phone calls. Back then, the phone rang, you had no idea who was calling, so you picked up and said, "Hello?" The call could be the love of your life, a family member, a friend, a frenemy, a telemarketer, a survey company, or a wrong number. But sometimes you'd receive a phone call from a stranger asking a question like, "Is your refrigerator running?" You'd answer, "Yes, it's running," and the giggling voice on the other end of the line would say, "You better go catch it!" It was the highest form of humor before internet memes were invented.

If you're old enough to remember those crank calls, then you may be old enough to have been alive when the last literal crank telephones were still in operation. Old-fashioned? Sure. Outdated? Absolutely. But they hung on in Woodstock right up until 1981. A testament to this town holding on to the old technology sits just across the street from the Woodstock Post Office in the form of a fourteen-foot-tall hand-crank telephone. How it got here was a long road.

Alexander Graham Bell made the first telephone call on March 10, 1876. The magic of the telephone is that it turns your voice into an electronic signal that travels over a wire and then gets converted back into sound. The technology was built off the telegraph, where an electric signal was transmitted across a wire, where it was converted into dots and dashes. So the wires were already there, Bell just took it to the next level.

The first people to adopt the telephone were businesses that could afford the new technology, but soon, private residences in urban areas started getting telephones, and then it spread.

The earliest phones were crank-type boxes. You turn the crank, which spins a magneto and sends an electric current to ring the bells on other phones in the same line. In coming years, that current alerted an operator at a switchboard, who would then patch your call through. Every phone in the line had its own pattern of rings so you knew if the incoming call was for you or not.

Rotary phones eventually replaced those old crank telephones, and in 1962, the first touch-tone phones were introduced. Around that same time, the number of telephone operators dwindled, as they were replaced by phone books and people direct-dialing numbers to the people they wished to call.

But not in Woodstock. The first phone system in town was installed in 1938 when Woodstock had only fifteen telephones. The Bryant Pond Telephone Company, owned by Barbara and Elden Hathaway, bought the system in 1951 and operated the business out of their home. At that time there were 431 customers on the old magneto system, but big changes were coming by 1981. The Oxford Telephone company bought the Bryant Pond Company with plans to update the whole system to new lines.

Two Woodstock locals, named Dave Perham and Brad Hooper, teamed up to form the "Don't Yank the Crank" committee. People don't like change. So a petition circulated asking

people to "prayerfully consider maintaining the present telephone system. It's hoped that this system will be preserved as an historic landmark for the Bryant Pond area and the State of Maine." The petition was placed in the village store.

It took only seven hours for the petition to reach ninety signatures in town. Members of the Don't Yank the Crank committee viewed their antiquated phone system the way San Francisco viewed its cable cars. It was something to be preserved—part of the town's identity.

The petition was sent to the Oxford Telephone Company and to a federal agency in hopes of getting an intervention from Washington, DC. No matter how quaint the request, however, progress can't be stopped. No intervention came. No minds were changed at the Oxford Telephone Company. The old system was phased out. At some point in 1981, someone in Woodstock turned the crank on their phone for the last time.

In 2008, this fourteen-foot giant crank telephone monument was placed in Remembrance Park. It was sculpted by Gil Whitman, a World War II veteran, a Maine state representative, and a barbershop quartet singer. There's a plaque on the front that reads:

> THIS SCULPTURE BY GIL WHITMAN IS DEDICATED TO THE MEMORY OF BARBARA AND ELDEN HATHAWAY, OWNERS OF THE BRYANT POND TELEPHONE COMPANY.

Given all of the new technology and modern caller ID, there's now no way to suggest to Woodstock locals that they chase after their running refrigerators.

The Hoodoo Hearse of Holden

HOLDEN, MAINE

Back in June of 1901, a news article made the rounds regarding a strange and cursed hearse from Holden. This was a weird case of Yankee ingenuity and frugality turned sour.

The story began in the late fall of 1896 in the small town of Holden, located just east of Bangor. In Bangor, a man had died, and the family wanted his body brought to a burial plot about forty miles south, in Brooksville, Maine, on the seacoast.

When a loved one dies, you want to send them off in the finest way possible—in Bangor, that meant the Holden Hearse. It was historic, storied, and legendary in every way. It was the fanciest hearse around. It was large, polished, and jet black in color. This horse-drawn carriage was the finest ride your deceased loved one could take.

The hearse was built in England in the late 1700s, so it was already more than a century old at the time. The hearse first arrived in Massachusetts and immediately drew the attention of a public who was just dying to get a closer look.

This large and fancy hearse carriage first went into service in Ipswich, Massachusetts, where it carted the deceased to their final burials. The hearse was in such high demand that it was earning revenues of close to $1,000 per year.

After twenty-five years of service in Ipswich, the hearse was sold to some business partners in New Wrentham, Maine, where

MAINE'S HOODOO HEARSE

An Ancient Vehicle That Made Trouble and Pointed the Way to Death.

From the New York Sun.

It is hoped now that the evil reputation that has marked the late career of the old Holden hearse has come to an end. The hearse was made in England more than a century ago and was brought over to Massachusetts as something unusual in the line of funeral splendor.

Having done its solemn duty in Ipswich, Mass., for nearly a quarter of a century it was sent down to New Wrentham, Me., and for seventy-five years was in constant demand for funerals in all parts of Hancock and Penobscot counties, often being sent more than fifty miles from home. The body of the carriage wore out four sets of wheels, and the revenues which it earned for its owners mounted up to almost $1,000 a year.

It had become the custom for the heaviest stockholders in the vehicle to drive the horse and attend all the funerals. Six

it continued to gain attention and earn a lot of money for its owners. And then in 1896, the town of Holden purchased the hearse for $700, using taxpayer money. Some locals invested in the hearse, because, of course, you still needed to pay a driver and care for the horses that pulled the dead sled.

Back to the fall of 1896. There had already been six hearse drivers who had gotten old and passed away since this stately carriage had first gone into service in New England over a century earlier. And now the seventh driver of this hearse had been asked to bring a casket from Bangor to Brooksville for burial.

When the driver finished his delivery in Brooksville, he discovered that the family of the deceased was too poor to pay his full fare. When you consider the time, feeding and boarding the horses, plus boarding the driver, the trip was going to be a financial loss. So, the driver came up with an idea.

Brooksville is right on Maine's coast. So the driver purchased six hundred pounds of salt codfish and used the hearse to bring it back to Holden for sale. Salt codfish was tough to get in landlocked Holden. The profits from the fish sales could help offset the losses the driver had suffered. But when he arrived back in Holden, some locals were appalled. They were furious! Carrying a cargo of dead fish in a hearse wasn't just disrespectful; it was sacrilegious! How could he!?

One indignant person told another, and suddenly this *thing* that wasn't really a *thing* . . . well . . . it became a *thing*.

Some of the Holden old-timers sent for their lawyers and updated their wills to stipulate that their mortal remains would *not* be conveyed in this sullied codfish carcass carriage!

This created a legal problem and nightmare for the town. This now-infamous hearse had contracts with two cemetery associations that stipulated that they were the hearse company hired for any burials in those cemeteries. So, if someone wanted to be buried in one of those cemeteries, and the deceased had updated their will to say, "Don't use this specific hearse," now they had a legal problem. If you wanted to be buried with your family in a certain cemetery, you had to use this hearse. If you didn't want to use that hearse, then you had to find somewhere else to be buried.

Some folks in town could care less about the hearse being used to carry cod. But others were digging in. We mean literally digging in. They began to fence off burial plots on their own land so they wouldn't need a cemetery or a hearse.

Holden was a town soon divided into two factions: The pro-hearse group and the hearse-haters. The fight continued throughout the winter of 1897. Then the courts ruled on the contracts in favor of the hearse. A contract is a contract, a fish delivery should be inconsequential from a legal standpoint. But the ruling did nothing to settle the dispute. In fact, it's worth mentioning that no one from the anti-hearse families had died in the six months since this feud started. They were *that* stubborn about not wanting to have their corpse ride in a hearse sullied by codfish.

Some folks in Holden owned financial shares in that hearse. Others were still offended that their favorite hearse had been ruined less than a year since it first went into service in town. That's when some of the boys from the hearse-hating side of town snuck into the old storage barn and wheeled the hearse to the front lawn of a hearse-supporting family to be found the next day when the sun came up.

A harmless enough prank, but then the strangest thing happened . . . a few days after the hearse was left on the yard of this family, one of the family members died. A coincidence, we're sure.

A month later, some kids pulled the same prank again. This time with a different pro-hearse family, still leaving it to be found in the front yard. And, soon after, a member of that pranked family died. Maybe a coincidence?

The third time the prank was pulled . . . okay, *not* a coincidence. Now we're talking local terror.

Some suggested they burn up this obviously cursed hearse and be done with it forever. But the pro-hearse faction of Holden was stubborn too. Burning it up would be like giving in. Losing. Even though the hearse wasn't in service anymore.

Holden decided to paint the hearse, give it a fresh coat of varnish, and then they tried to sell it for almost any price. But it was too late. Given the reputation, no one wanted it. So the hearse remained locked away for good, and the story made the wire service under the headline: "The Hoodoo Hearse."

Maine's Sistine Chapel

SOUTH SOLON, MAINE

Built in 1842 and officially called the South Solon Meeting House, locals know this place better as the "Sistine Chapel of Maine."

From the outside, the building looks like countless other meetinghouses throughout New England, but stepping inside is like walking into a painting. There are simple wooden pews and a wooden pulpit, but everything is painted in vibrant colors.

In the 1950s, the Skowhegan School of Painting and Sculpture held a competition for their students to paint frescos on the walls of the meetinghouse. The only guidance was that this was a religious building. Otherwise, they had free rein. The result: a rainbow of imagery, from farm fields to the face of Jesus looking down upon you.

The student artists left enough of an impression that their work has been preserved by the South Solon Historical Society ever since.

Hymns of the Christian Life
Hymns of the Christian Life

Maine's Stolen Governor

AUGUSTA, MAINE

Maine's Statehouse in Augusta looks almost like a cross between the White House and the Capitol building in Washington, DC. It's formal. It's got gravitas. You can imagine how Maine's governor must feel gazing across the street at Capital Park with its lines of trees, park benches, memorials, and, of course, a single tomb residing in that park—a tomb for one of the governor's predecessors: Governor Enoch Lincoln, as well as a couple of other notable Maine forefathers.

Government buildings are full of bureaucracies. Sometimes civil workers lose things, like paperwork, forms, records, phone numbers, reimbursement checks, the decaying corpse of a former governor, pens, tax returns, deeds to properties, legal filings. You know, mistakes that can happen to anyone.

Capital Park's lone tomb is marked with an obelisk and a small wrought-iron fence. Built into the side of a hill facing the capitol building, it's the tomb of Maine's sixth governor, Enoch Lincoln, plus three others: a former state senator, a state representative, and a House clerk. The inscription reads: LINCOLN OF PORTLAND. GOVERNOR OF MAINE. DIED OCTOBER 8, 1829. AGE 40.

The only problem is—*and it's only a minor problem, really*—the governor's body is *not* inside anymore.

Enoch Lincoln was born in 1788 in Worcester, Massachusetts. A creative kid, he loved to read and write, and his parents saw to it that he received a good education. After graduating from Harvard in 1807, Enoch turned to law and politics. He began practicing law in Salem, Massachusetts, in 1811, then served as a United States district attorney before moving to Paris, Massachusetts—which would later become a town in Maine when Maine achieved statehood in 1820.

During this time, Lincoln was also pursuing his other passion: writing. In 1816, Enoch published a two-thousand-line poem titled *The Village*. Though the poem was written in rhyming verse, Lincoln used his words to comment on social reforms, such as women's rights and the abolition of slavery, and he addressed his views on nature, and all kinds of other subjects relative to small-town New England life during his time.

When Maine achieved statehood in 1820, Lincoln served as one of the new state's first representatives to Congress. He was a charming guy, and his political career was just warming up. The newspapers described him as "fine, clear eyes, pleasant mouth, sanguine complexion, and golden hair." Though many women were infatuated with the charming, charismatic, and successful poet/politician, no love caught his eye. He remained focused on his career.

In 1827, at thirty-seven years of age, the unmarried Lincoln was elected the sixth Governor of Maine. Back then, governor was a one-year term. Still, the people of Maine loved him, and he was reelected again the following year, and the year after that.

Enoch Lincoln was part of the decision to make Augusta Maine's capital, he worked to improve education for all the

children of the state because he understood that investments in education pay off big-time down the road, and the people of Maine liked him enough to name a town after him, which he approved.

On July 4, 1829, Governor Lincoln oversaw the ceremony to lay the cornerstone of the brand-new capitol building in Augusta, complete with "imposing Masonic ceremonies, a procession of the Governor and Council and the Grand Lodge of Maine being escorted to the site by the Augusta Light Infantry."

Sadly, the governor never got the chance to see the finished capitol because by September 1829, Lincoln took ill. On September 30, though weak, Lincoln delivered an address to the students of the Coney Female Academy at Augusta. The following day he was confined to bed rest. It was a bed he wouldn't leave again. Not in life, anyway. He relayed to his friends during his illness that he understood this was his end. On Tuesday, October 8, 1829, Governor Enoch Lincoln died at age forty.

After Enoch's passing in 1829, his body was laid to rest on public grounds in the park across the street from Augusta's under-construction capitol building. In 1842, a more formal crypt and monument were constructed on the same site so Governor Lincoln could rest in a dignified manner alongside a couple of other notable Maine politicians who were also given this tomb of honor. This is where our story *should* end . . . but it doesn't.

By 1903, Lincoln's tomb was getting rough around the edges, so the legislators of Maine set aside a little budget money to clean it up and make repairs to the stones. According to 1903 documents, when the tomb was opened, Governor Lincoln's metal casket was observed as "holding up well," but the caskets of the other people buried inside—namely, a state senator and state representative and a House clerk—were rotting away, so their remains were placed in new caskets. Here's another place where our story *should* end . . . but it didn't.

By the 1950s, more Maine budget money was set aside to clean up the tomb area and make some improvements. A little spit and polish, and the site was dignified once again.

If we jump ahead again, this time to 1986, the state of Maine performed a routine inspection of the tomb to look for signs of weathering. They cleaned out the beer cans and took care of minor maintenance. But when they opened the door to the tomb to look inside, they noticed something strange. The tomb . . . was empty.

One of the strangest parts of this story is that the workers who made this discovery managed to keep it pretty quiet for a while. The story didn't blow up until November 1991, when a writer from the Associated Press got wind of the news and did some research and reporting. The article described how Sheila McKenna, a history specialist at the state library, followed the paper trail to try to figure out who had removed the bodies and where they would have gone, but she found nothing. McKenna's best guess was that during one of the routine inspections or cleanups, some workers removed the caskets and maybe forgot to put them back in again?

The Allagash UFO Incident

ALLAGASH WILDERNESS, MAINE

In August of 1976, four young men were taking a camping trip up to the Allagash Wilderness in northern Maine. Brothers Jack and Jim Weiner, Chuck Rak, and Charlie Foltz all attended the Massachusetts College of Art and Design and had been planning this two-week camping trip for a while.

The first day of the camping trip was mostly uneventful. They paddled their canoes up the Allagash Wilderness Waterway until they found a place to make camp near the river. But the second night the men made camp, something strange happened.

The four were sitting around a campfire when Jim Weiner noticed a strange light in the sky. It was too bright to be a star, it was too bright to be an airplane, and it wasn't streaking across the sky like a meteorite. He watched the light for about thirty seconds and then it was gone.

Two nights later, on August 20, after making camp they paddled their canoe onto the water to do some night fishing. They had built a good-sized campfire to serve as a beacon to find their way back. The four friends had been out on the water no more than fifteen minutes when a bright light appeared in the sky again. Chuck Rak used his flashlight to try to signal Morse Code to the craft. Whatever intelligence was behind the light in the sky soon took notice of the men in the canoe. They suddenly found themselves surrounded by a beam of light like a spotlight. They were nervous and began rowing for shore, but the light followed them. It took only a minute or two for them to reach their camp and pull their boat onto shore. That's when the light vanished, and the sky was once again empty. But most curious was that their campfire had burned down to glowing embers.

This shouldn't have been possible. The fire they built should have burned for hours. They figured they were gone no more than twenty minutes. Confused, they found themselves asking if they were gone minutes or hours. Nothing made sense.

Jumping ahead twelve years, brothers Jack and Jim Weiner were experiencing strange nightmares where they found themselves naked and sitting on a bench with their old friends Chuck Rak and Charlie Foltz. In the dream, they were scared of something. Jack and Jim sought out UFO researcher Ray Fowler who suggested maybe they had suppressed a memory from their camping trip to the Allagash. All four agreed to undergo hypnosis. That's when they claimed they recalled memories of being abducted onto a ship.

Fowler published their story in the 1993 book *The Allagash Abductions*. Years later, Rak would claim they made up most of the story for money and notoriety (though there's little of either to be gained sharing these kinds of stories). Rak said he remembers seeing the lights in the sky, but not being abducted. The other three have stuck to their story, giving us all one more thing to worry about when it comes to remote camping trips deep in the woods of Maine.

A Nerve Tonic That Launched a War

UNION, MAINE

In July of 1865, Augustin Thompson had just finished serving in the Union Army in the Civil War. He was part of the contingent of men guarding the coast by the key shipbuilding city of Bath, Maine.

Thompson was born in 1835 and raised in Union, Maine. After serving in the war, he attended Hahnemann Homeopathic College in Philadelphia, where he learned to practice medicine. With a medical degree in hand, he returned to New England and settled in Lowell, Massachusetts.

By 1876, Dr. Thompson's medical practice had grown. He was a sought-after doctor in his region. Eager to leave his mark on the world of medicine, he began to tinker with elixirs, plant roots, and other ingredients to develop his own medicine. He was trying to come up with a formula that could cure just about anything.

Snake oil, you say? Not so fast. You need to remember that many medical innovations came about during the US Civil War (1861–1865). Lives were saved with new amputation methods, and the anesthesia inhaler was invented to sedate people while they underwent lifesaving surgeries. Then there were morphine, chloroform, ether, and other chemicals finding medical uses. It was a new era of medicine. Discoveries were being made all the time. Dr. Thompson started experimenting with a South American plant called gentian root. It has a bitter taste, but, when mixed properly, some of his patients felt better.

Dr. Thompson wasn't just a student of medicine, he was enterprising. And pretty soon, he came up with an elixir he claimed was effective against "paralysis, softening of the brain, nervousness, and insomnia."

He called this tonic *Moxie Nerve Food*, including the word *moxie*, which he'd heard growing up in Maine. It's an Abenaki word that means, "dark water." There are ponds, streams, and falls bearing this name in Maine. Dr. Thompson thought it was a good fit . . . but then again, he also thought maybe that origin story wasn't sexy enough, so another version of the story suggested he named his tonic after a lieutenant he served with in the Civil War, a man who discovered the medical uses for gentian root.

No matter the origin of the name, Dr. Thompson peddled his tonic for several years around the city of Lowell. His reputation grew. It seemed that everyone was knocking on his door for his medical advice and his elixir. Though most medicine tastes bad, not his "nerve food." Folks liked the blend of sweetness and bitterness. And pretty soon, he was selling the stuff by the case. Whether the elixir was actually curing people or they just liked the flavor didn't seem to matter too much. The bottles flew off his shelves.

In 1884, Dr. Thompson added an ingredient that not only caused an explosion in sales, but would ultimately be the first shot fired in an upcoming war . . . he added soda water and changed the name to *Beverage Moxie Nerve Food*. When Thompson applied for a patent in 1885, he explained that it was "a liquid preparation charged with soda for the cure of paralysis, softening of the brain,

JACK & KATHLEEN ALGEO
HIGGINS FAMILY
YOU GOT MOXIE!
MOXIE
TRADE MARK REG. U.S. PAT. OFFICE
A Compound for the Nervous System also a Delicious
Healthful Beverage
THE MOXIE COMPANY
SOLE PROPRIETORS AND MANUFACTURERS
BOSTON
MOXIE
MOXIE
MOXIE CAFE
DRINK
MOXIE
THE MOXIE COMPANY
DRINK
MOXIE

and mental imbecility." At that point he also began selling the stuff in bulk as soda fountain syrup.

In May of 1886, Dr. John S. Pemberton, a pharmacist down in Atlanta, Georgia, heard about Dr. Thompson's nerve tonic, so he created a syrup for his soda fountain. That product would soon be known as Coca-Cola. But Coca-Cola sales weren't even close to those of Moxie during those early days of the soda wars.

Dr. Augustin Thompson died in June of 1903. But that wasn't the end of Moxie. The soda wars were just beginning.

Down in Atlanta, Coca-Cola sales were exploding everywhere. By the 1920s, after its initial public offering, Coke was a clear cola juggernaut, but folks in New England still liked their Moxie.

Battle lines were being drawn in the soda wars. The soda you drank became part of how you defined yourself. People made it public who they endorsed and who they did not. In the 1920s, Coca-Cola was now the big dog, but President Calvin Coolidge? He loved Moxie.

Once Red Sox legend Ted Williams started endorsing Moxie on the radio and in print ads, that sealed it. New England's got Moxie! Around that time, the word *moxie* entered the English lexicon to mean spunk. Nerve. Character. It's a word that traces its roots to an elixir invented by a guy from Union, Maine.

On May 10, 2005, Moxie was designated the official soft drink of Maine, and the word is still used to refer to spunk and courage.

Though Coca-Cola may have decisively won the soda wars (Coca-Cola bought Moxie in 2018), no one has ever said, "That kid showed some real Coca-Cola in that fight." Nope. He showed Moxie.

The Leaping Lumberjacks of Central Maine

MOOSEHEAD LAKE, MAINE

During the 19th century, the United States was expanding and building with bold ambition. Homes, businesses, civil projects, and everything in between needed lumber, and lots of it. The state of Maine had plenty of it. They just needed lumberjacks to come fell these trees and move them to the lumberyards.

There was a saying in Maine's lumberjack camps that there were always three shifts: those working, those quitting, and those coming to take the open jobs. Due to demand and turnover, Maine needed all the able-bodied folks they could find. Opportunities abounded if you could swing an axe, and that drew plenty of men down from Canada to find work.

When a group of French-Canadian lumberjacks showed up at camp looking for jobs, the foreman didn't ask too many questions. If you could swing an axe and keep up, good enough.

Teasing greenhorns came with the territory out there in the woods. At the end of a hard day there wasn't much to do besides swap stories by the fire and tease the new guys. Then a strange discovery was made. One of the veteran lumberjacks snuck up behind one of the French-Canadian newbies and gave him a scare. That's when the greenhorn began leaping up and down over and over and over while screaming.

The veteran lumberjack expected a jump out of the new guy, but nothing like this. No one in camp had ever seen anything like it. You might think that, after this event, the other lumberjacks figured, *We should lay off these guys, considering their odd affliction.* But you'd be wrong. With little else for entertainment out there in the woods, these French-Canadian greenhorns became the equivalent of a Broadway musical.

Not only was it discovered that, once startled, these new guys would leap up and down screaming, but they were also highly susceptible to influence when in this excited state. So you could tell them to do things like, "Go jump in the river," and they would.

As word of this odd phenomenon spread, it was soon learned that other French-Canadian loggers hailing from a specific region of Quebec also suffered from the same strange affliction.

Pretty soon the story caught the attention of Dr. George Miller Beard. Dr. Beard was a neurologist who studied the startle reflex. He was born in Connecticut, educated in New York City, but once he heard the stories from the lumber camps, he raced to Maine to study this phenomenon for himself. Dr. Beard observed the prank and wrote about it: "When told to strike, he strikes, when told to throw it, he throws it, whatever he has in his hands. He repeated or echoed the sound of the word as it came to him, in a quick sharp voice, at the same time he jumped, or struck, or threw, or raised his shoulders, or made some other violent muscular motion. They could not help repeating the word or sound that came from the person that ordered them."

Dr. Beard published his findings in newspapers and scholarly journals. His work eventually reached a French neurologist who also studied involuntary neurological responses with people. The French neurologist believed that this Leaping Logger syndrome was simply a tic that was part of a broader issue. The name of this French neurologist was Georges Gilles de la Tourette . . . the man who named Tourette's syndrome.

The Specter Moose of Lobster Lake

PISCATAQUIS, MAINE

A ghost? Check. A monster? Check. A moose? Check. A place called "Lobster Lake"? Check. This may be the most *New England Legends*-y headline ever written. And it's a legend that's been around since 1891.

In December of 1900, the newspapers picked up a sighting report of this legendary moose. It read:

> The enormous moose that has been the wonder of the sportsmen in northern Maine since 1891 has again been seen, and this time under rather different circumstances from ever before. A bicyclist came close to the monster in the road between Sherman and Macwahoc, and was obliged to abandon his wheels and climb a tree for safety. So he had a near view of the animal.
>
> Every story that comes from the north woods concerning this moose makes him a little bigger than before. It is generally believed that no moose ever killed anyone in Maine, or, so far as is known, anywhere else. And none has approached in stature or weight, much less in spread of antlers, this specter moose of Lobster Lake. He is called the "specter moose" because of the weird appearance he presents at night—a dirty gray.

In 1891, Clarence Duffy of Old Town, Maine, was serving as a guide around Lobster Lake when he first spotted the giant white moose. When Duffy told others what he'd seen, they laughed at him. But then there were other sightings in coming years—all of them near Lobster Lake.

In 1899, Gilman Brown of West Newbury, Massachusetts, got closer to the beast than any other witness. Brown claimed the moose stood fifteen feet high with antlers ten to twelve feet across. He reported that he was close enough to count twenty-two points on one side of his antlers. He took a shot at the moose with his rifle, but couldn't bring it down.

To give you some perspective, according to Maine's Department of Inland Fisheries and Wildlife, the largest bull moose ever shot in Maine weighed about 1,767 pounds with a length of nine feet and a height of about six feet measured at the shoulders.

The Specter Moose of Lobster Lake has been described as weighing at least 2,500 pounds and standing fifteen feet tall.

An albino moose is rare, but it happens. A moose that's albino and also twice as large as the largest moose ever shot in Maine has never been proven. As the newspaper account stated, each description of the beast makes it slightly larger than the previous one. The conclusion was that it must be a real animal, and if a hunter could bring it down, fame and fortune would await.

Was this specter moose a real flesh-and-blood animal? Or could it have been something more *unnatural*, which explains why no hunter could bring it down? And if that's the case, is it still out there?

Razor Shins

AROOSTOOK COUNTY, MAINE

Tales of Razor Shins go back at least two centuries. He's been described as a Native American in full war dress; however, where his lower legs should be are two blades as sharp as any sword you'd care to test. If Razor Shins is angry, he may run up to you and swing his leg level with your head and then . . . well, it's too late. It's over for you. Razor Shins *must* be appeased.

The legend of Razor Shins got a huge boost around the fires of logging camps in the woods of Maine, especially during the 19th century when Maine was producing more lumber than anywhere else in the northeastern United States.

Job turnover among loggers was high. Some loggers were injured and needed to be replaced, others saved enough money for whatever they planned to buy and moved on, and some had enough of the tough conditions and sought their fortunes someplace else.

As new greenhorns came into the camps, they quickly learned what was expected of them. They were also told the story of Razor Shins, and how it was critical for new loggers to leave a jug of booze outside of their tent in those first nights in a new camp. Preferably whiskey or rum. If you left out the booze, in the morning the jug would be empty, and Razor Shins would leave you alone. He might even help you take down a tree or two in your section if he was feeling generous. However, fail to leave out the booze and you could be in mortal danger. Accidents happened out there in the deep woods.

For decades, the legend of Razor Shins was passed from logger to logger throughout the camps. Sometimes stories of loggers dying in accidents would later be attributed to an angry Razor Shins. It's not lost on us that the story kept a steady supply of free booze flowing to the veterans of the camp.

Razor Shins was famous enough that when the year 1920 rolled around and Prohibition made alcohol illegal nationwide, the *Boston Globe* ran a headline that read: "Will Razor Shins Survive When His Supply of Rum Is Cut Off?"

Logging camps are a thing of the past, as is Prohibition. Without the many loggers and logging camps, Razor Shins has surely faded, but he'll never go away entirely as long as someone still fells a tree in the woods of Maine.

The Pamola

MT. KATAHDIN, MAINE

At 5,267 feet tall, Mt. Katahdin is the highest peak in Maine. It also marks the end (or beginning) of the 2,200-mile-long Appalachian Trail that runs to Spring Mountain in northern Georgia. Katahdin is legendary not just for its size and significance for those who trek the A.T.; it's legendary because its summit is guarded by a beast called Pamola.

Pamola has the body of a man, but giant wings like an eagle and the head of a moose. According to the Penobscot Indians who lived in central Maine for centuries, the Pamola is the god of thunder. He dwells near the top because you're not supposed to go up there. After all, it's dangerous. There are few natural resources, and those who dare to thumb their nose at the warnings and the stories sometimes perish up there because weather conditions can deteriorate quickly.

In 1864, American author and literary treasure Henry David Thoreau published a book called *The Maine Woods*. In it, he explored this region and wrote about this very beast.

The tops of mountains are among the unfinished parts of the globe, whither it is a slight insult to the gods to climb and pry into their secrets, and test their effect on our humanity. Only daring and insolent men, perchance, go there. Simple races, as savages, do not climb mountains—their tops are sacred and mysterious tracts, never visited by humans. Pamola is always angry with those who climb to the summit of Katahdin.

By most descriptions, Pamola is a thunderbird (save for the head of a moose, but that could be Maine putting her thumbprint on a legend that spans the country). Mythology is filled with stories of half-human/half-animals. The god Zeus had companions in battle. One of those was a group of siblings who were described as half-human/half-birds, the most famous being the goddess Nike.

In Native American mythology, stories abound of men with wings that spanned so wide when they flapped it would create a sound like thunder (thus the name). The United States Air Force believed in the story enough to adorn the bottom of their air demonstration squadron of F-16s with the mythical beast and name the group the Thunderbirds. We can only hope that when the squadron flies over Maine, they add in the head of the moose for some local color.

OPERA HOUSE

The Phantom of the Opera House

BOOTHBAY, MAINE

Built in 1894, the Opera House at Boothbay Harbor has served many roles, including a school gym, indoor mall, entertainment center, music hall, meeting house—everything but, ironically, a place for opera. The building was constructed by the Knights of Pythias, a somewhat secretive fraternal group, who held their meetings on the second floor (where women were never allowed) and leased the rest of the space out to the town for civic use. Still, with well over a century of human activity behind it, the Opera House has earned a haunted reputation.

At the turn of the 20th century, few movies made it out to Boothbay Harbor. Entertainment came in the form of traveling vaudeville acts, plays, bands, and wrestling matches. Touring artists would make their way up the coast via steamboats, make some money at the Opera House, then move on. The Opera House was a place for everything from high school proms to funerals to town meetings.

While some haunts have a few prominent spirits, the ghosts of this building seem to be more transient in nature—which makes sense, considering how many people came and went over the decades.

A popular ghostly tale people recount about this Opera House involves a piano on the second floor that's been known to play by itself. The staff here are quick to point out that there's some truth to this legend . . . it is, after all, a player piano. Though none of the current staff have witnessed the piano playing by paranormal forces, they have witnessed other unexplained events.

One manager has heard footsteps on the stairwells when she was alone in the building; others have heard singing and music when there were no performances happening. The ghost of a little boy has been reported in the balcony, and a ghostly couple have been spotted on the third floor.

Today, this building is still a place for entertainment and productions that bring in large crowds. With all the nonstop human activity here, one would expect they will never run out of ghosts. We take comfort in that.

The Hermit of Manana Island

MONHEGAN ISLAND, MAINE

Manana Island is small and isolated. It's about eighteen hundred feet long and a thousand feet wide. There's nary a tree to be found, just some bushes, rocks, and grass. For forty years this tiny island was home to a single resident: Ray Phillips, better known as the Hermit of Manana Island.

Manana Island sits just a few hundred feet from its bigger brother island, Monhegan, which boasts about sixty-four residents year-round, though that number swells in the summer tourist season. The old-timers today fondly remember their neighbor across the water.

Ray Phillips was born in Maine and served as a soldier during World War I, but was injured in battle seriously enough to receive a lifetime government pension. After the war, he attended the University of Maine, where he earned average grades. Then after graduating he moved down to New York City to live with his mother, who earned her living as a fortune teller. Ray Phillips found work as a teacher and food inspector, and though the 1920s were roaring for everyone else, they weren't for Phillips. He wasn't dating anyone. Never married. No children. He wasn't one for wild parties or anything like that. When the stock market crashed in 1929, he watched as the Great Depression ushered in a rough time for the whole nation. Phillips saw breadlines in New York. He saw suffering everywhere he looked. One day in 1931 he had enough. So he bought a small boat and sailed it north.

He followed the shore until he found a place called Monhegan Island. It's still Maine, so somewhat familiar, but ten miles from shore, so you really couldn't see the mainland. With so few people it was almost perfect. After fishing the coast of Monhegan for a few years and saving his money, he had saved enough to buy one-sixth of the island across the water. He sailed his boat over, found some driftwood, and started building his shack.

And so the hermit's new life began. Plenty of washed-up driftwood and lumber gave Phillips materials to build additions onto his shack, and each month he received $109 from his veteran's pension and $77 from his social security. When he needed supplies, he rowed his boat across the strait and bought what he needed in Monhegan.

Some of those supplies included sheep. The sheep could graze on the island, and in the colder months, Phillips discovered an incredible heat source: bringing the sheep inside his shack. With the sheep and himself in such a tight space, it was plenty warm, even in Maine's rough winters.

Over time, he built more additions onto his shack, plus a system to collect rainwater for drinking and cleaning because his shack had no running water or electricity. He lit his humble dwelling with oil and kerosene lamps.

When summer and the tourists came, the sheep slept outside. Summer after summer, more tourists noticed the man across the way with the sheep and the strange shack. Pretty soon,

some rowed over to meet him. Phillips was always friendly to his visitors. He was happy to chat or pose for a picture, and his reputation grew.

As happens to hermits, others think maybe he has some divine insight, so journalists came to ask questions, and his legend grew. He received fan mail from people around the country. And he often wrote back, using the backs of the letters written to him.

By 1975, the eighty-three-year-old Ray Phillips was struggling to keep up with his chores. After falling into the frigid water, he caught pneumonia. His friends on Monhegan Island begged him to go to the mainland to a hospital, but the old hermit refused. The best he offered was to place a kerosene lamp in his window each night so the folks across the water knew he was okay.

On May 4, 1975, there was no light in the window. Phillips had passed away, and Manana Island has sat vacant ever since.

The Billdad

SKINNER, MAINE

There's no question that Maine loggers helped build the country. During periods of rapid expansion, America needed wood to build houses, and Maine had tons of it. When sitting around the logging camps after swinging an axe all day, loggers had little to do but share stories. The tales were as tall as the trees, but there was always some inherent moral or lesson to them. Often the moral had to do with being careful doing this most dangerous work.

Back in 1910, William T. Cox published a collection of some of the various tales told in the logging camps of America. The book is titled *Fearsome Creatures of the Lumberwoods*. One of his stories from Maine is worth passing along:

If you have ever paddled around Boundary Pond, in northwest Maine, at night you have probably heard from out the black depths of a cove a spat like a paddle striking the water. It may have been a paddle, but the chances are ten to one that it was a billdad fishing. This animal occurs only on this one pond, in Hurricane Township. It's about the size of a beaver, but has long, kangaroo-like hind legs, short front legs, webbed feet, and a heavy, hawk-like bill. Its mode of fishing is to crouch on a grassy point overlooking the water, and when a trout rises for a bug, to leap with amazing swiftness just past the fish, bringing its heavy, flat tail down with a resounding smack over him. This stuns the fish, which is immediately picked up and eaten by the billdad. It has been reported that sixty yards is an average jump for an adult male.

Up to three years ago the opinion was current among lumberjacks that the billdad was fine eating, but since the beasts are exceedingly shy and hard to catch no one was able to remember having tasted the meat. That fall, one was killed on Boundary Pond and brought into the Great Northern Paper Company's camp on Hurricane Lake, where the cook made a most savory slumgullion of it. The first and only man to taste

it was Bill Murphy, a toe-road swamper from Ambajejus. After the first mouthful his body stiffened, his eyes glazed, and his hands clutched the table edge. With a wild yell, he rushed out of the cookhouse, down to the lake, and leaped clear out fifty yards, coming down in a sitting posture—exactly like a billdad catching a fish. Of course, he sank like a stone. Since then, not a lumberjack in Maine will touch billdad meat, not even with a pike pole.

The moral:

Don't eat every animal you find in the wild . . . or else!

Index

A

Abenaki people, 173, 187–188, 206
Adams, Albert, 76–77
Adams, Isaac, 87–89
Albany, New Hampshire, 92–94
Allagash Wilderness, Maine, 205
Allen, Ayres B., 180
Allen, Ethan, 178–180
Alvarez, Bren, 162–164
Amun-Her-Khepesh-Ef, mummy of, 170
antisemitism, 47
Appalachian Trail, 98, 213
armored skeleton, 62
Aroostook County, Maine, 211
Asselin, Ted, 78–80
Augusta, Maine, 202–204
Avery, John and Mitt, 194
Ayer, A. D., 35–36

B

Babson, Roger, 54–57
baked beans and the Devil, 107–109
Ball, Harvey, 57–59
Bancroft, Charles, 103
Bangor, Maine, 192, 197–198
Bantam Lake, Connecticut, 17
Barker, Kim, 97
Barnum, P. T., 12, 14, 174
Barton, Nancy, 110–113
Battis, Edward, 52
Battle of the Frogs, 8–10
Beard, George Miller, 209–210
beard, persecuted for wearing a, 46–47
beasts
  billdad, 218–219
  Burning Beast of Glocester, 142–143
  Champ, the Lake Monster, 173–175, 178
  Glawackus, 25–27
  Gungywamp, 32–34
  Ice Age frog, 181
  Pamola, 213
  Razor Shins, 211
  Sleeping Giant, 10–12
  specter moose of Lobster Lake, 210–211
  Wampahoofus, 167
  Woonsocket werewolf, 138–139
  See also sea serpents
bed warmers, 70
Beer Bottle Church, New Hampshire, 90–91
Bell, Alexander Graham, 195
Bell, Sally, 65
Bellows Falls, Vermont, 187–188
Ben and Jerry's Flavor Graveyard, Vermont, 164–166
Bennington, Vermont, 180
Benton, Thomas (Doc), 98–99
Berkshire County, Massachusetts, 64–65
billdad, 218–219
Billings, Richard, 131, 133
Bitter, Karl, 160–161
Black Agnes, 160–161
black dog of Meriden, 27–29
Blackstone River, 138–139
Bonvouleir, Joseph, 25
Boothbay, Maine, 214–215
Borden, Lizzie, 44–46
Boston, Massachusetts
  Great Molasses Flood, 47–49
  Old North Church rope flying, 66–68
  tea kettle, 53
  UFO sighting, 71
Boston Neck on Narragansett Bay, 154–156
boulders
  America's Stonehenge, 116–119
  Chicken Farmer sign, 84–86
  Dogtown's inspirational, 54–57
  and landslide disaster, 97
  See also rock carvings

Brandon, Vermont, 181
Brattleboro, Vermont, 184–185
Brattleboro Retreat Tower, 184–185
Bretton Woods, New Hampshire, 80–81
Bridgeport, Connecticut, 4–5
bridges
  Emily's Bridge (Gold Brook Bridge), 158–159
  over Willimantic River, and Battle of the Frogs, 8–10
  Vilas Bridge, Vermont, 187–188
Brimstone Hill, New Hampshire, 90
Brooksville, Maine, 197, 198
Brown, Caleb R., 135, 137
Brown, Gilman, 210
Brown, Rufus, Jr., 194
Brown-Tuttle settlement, Maine, 194
Bryant, William Cullen, 160–161
Bryant Pond Telephone Company, 195–197
Buck, Jonathan, 193–194
Bucksport, Maine, 193–194
Buff Ledge Camp, Vermont, 178
Bunyan, Paul, 192
Burlington, Vermont, 162–164, 178–180
Burning Beast of Glocester, 142–143
Burnside, Ambrose, 123
Burr, John, 4

C

Cape Elizabeth, Maine, 190–191
Carlson, Suzanne O., 149
castles
  Brattleboro Retreat Tower, 184–185
  Castle Craig, Hanging Hills of Meriden, 27–29
  ruins of Madame Sherri's summer castle, 114–115
cat meat, 131, 133
Cavendish, Vermont, 172–173
cemeteries
  Ben and Jerry's Flavor Graveyard, Vermont, 164–166
  of Bucksport, Maine, 193–194
  Cedar Grove Cemetery, New London, Connecticut, 21
  Cranston Hospital for the Insane, Rhode Island, 135–137
  Dummerston Center Cemetery, Vermont, 175–177
  Evergreen Cemetery, Leominster, Massachusetts, 46–47
  Evergreen Cemetery, New Haven, Vermont, 168–170
  Green Mount Cemetery, Burlington, Vermont, 178–180
  Green Mount Cemetery, Montpelier, Vermont, 160–161
  Liberty Hill Cemetery, Lebanon, Connecticut, 18
  Lowell Cemetery, Massachusetts, 50–51
  Notre Dame Cemetery, Worchester, Massachusetts, 57–59
  Old Stratfield Cemetery, Bridgeport, Connecticut, 4–5
  Rhode Island Historic Cemetery 17, 126–127
  Rhode Island Historic Cemetery 65, 148
  Second Burial Ground, New London, Connecticut, 21–23
  Selee Cemetery, Massachusetts, 59–61
  West Cemetery, Middlebury, Vermont, 170
  See also headstones
Chace, Lavinia, 126–127
Champ, the Lake Monster, 173–175, 178
Champlain, Samuel de, 173–174
Champlain Parkway, 162–164
Chase, Henry, 62
Chesterfield, New Hampshire, 114–115
Chicken Farmer I Still Love You, 84–86
Childs, John, 67–68
churches, 66–68, 76–77, 90–91, 200–201
Civilian Conservation Corps, 156
coal shipment, 70–71
Coca-Cola, 208
Coen, Joel, 25
Cohen, Ben, 164–166
Colbath, Ruth and Thomas, 93–94
Colchester, Vermont, 178
Conimicut Lighthouse, Rhode Island, 140–142
Connecticut, vi, 3
Connecticut River, 185, 187
Constitution State, 3
consumption. *See* tuberculosis
Continental dollars, 70
Cook, Hannah Borden, 62
Coolidge, Calvin, 208
Cornell, Janet, 178
Cox, William T., 218
Cranston, Rhode Island, 135–137
Cranston Hospital for the Insane, 135
Crawford, Ethan, 95
Crawford House, 110
Crawford Notch, New Hampshire, 82–84, 95–97, 110–113
Cumberland, Rhode Island, 126–127
curses
  of Black Agnes, 160–161
  black dog of Meriden, 27–29
  of cemetery vine, 175–177
  Devil Hole, 139
  of Hoodoo Hearse, 199
  of witch on Jonathan Buck, 193–194
Cutter, Calvin and Caroline, 76–77

D

Darey, George, 65
Darey's Pond, Massachusetts, 64–65
Darn Man, The, 35–36
Dartmouth College students, 98–99
DeLauro, Rosa, 17
Dennis, Lydia, 131, 133
Devil
  and baked beans at Purgatory Falls, 107–109
  contract with, 100–103
  and Purgatory Chasm, 152–153
Devil Hole, 139
Dexter, Timothy, 68–71
Dodge, Carl, 185
dog, black, of Meriden, 27–29
Dogtown's boulders, 54–57
Don't Yank the Crank Committee, 195–197
Draper, Joseph, 184–185
Duffy, Clarence, 210
Dukakis, Michael, 64

E

earthquake of 1727, 90
East Berkshire, Vermont, 187
East Dummerston, Vermont, 175–177
Easton, Massachusetts, 59–61
Eastport, Maine, 189
Egyptian mummy, 170
Emily's Bridge, Vermont, 158–159
English Jack, 82–84
equinoxes, 32, 34, 117
Exeter, Rhode Island, 148
explosion on streetcar, 134

F

Fall River, Massachusetts, 44–46, 62–63
Fell, Barry, 117
Ferriere, Joe, 151
Ferry, Pelton, 25
filing cabinet tower, 162–164
fish in a hearse, 198–199
fisherwoman, Little Maggie, 185–187

fishing mode of a billdad, 218–219
Fiske, John, 3
floods
Great Molasses Flood, 47–49
and landslide disaster, 95–97
Foltz, Charlie, 205
fork in the road, 42–44, 224
Foster, Rhode Island, 146–147
Fowler, Ray, 205
Francestown, New Hampshire, 103–107
French-Canadians, 138–139, 209–210
frogs, 8–10, 181
Fuller, John G., 122

G

Gaffney, Matthew, 52
Gage, Phineas, 172–173
Gardiner, William, 155
Gardner Lake, Connecticut, 36–38
ghost ship of New Haven Harbor, 30–32
ghosts
of Bill Knights, 194
of Carolyn Stickney, 80–81
of Madame Sherri, 114–115
in Mark Twain's haunted mansion, 7
of Nancy Barton, 110–113
of Nellie Smith, 142
of nurse Mary, 183
of Opera House, 215
of Peleg Walker, 146–147
See also hauntings
ghouls (grave robbers), 135–137
Glastonbury, Connecticut, 25–27
Glawackus, 25–27
Glocester, Rhode Island, 142–143
Gloucester, Massachusetts, 51–52, 54–57
gorilla statue, Queen Connie, 170
grave robbing, 135–137
Gray, Sluman and Sarah, 18–19
Great Depression, 54
Great Falls National Bank, New Hampshire, 100–103
Great Molasses Flood, 47–49
Great Northern Paper Company, 218–219
Great Wall of Sandwich, New Hampshire, 87–89
Greenfield, Jerry, 164–166
Groton, Connecticut, 32–34
Gungywamp, 32–34
Gunn, Sir James, 40

H

Hall, Benjamin, 188
hamburger, first in nation, 15–17
Hamden, Connecticut, 10–12
Hamel, Gretchen Rule, 84, 86
Hampton, Connecticut, 35–36
Hampton Falls, New Hampshire, 90–91
Hanging Hills of Meriden, Connecticut, 27–29
Hartford, Connecticut, 6–7
Hathaway, Barbara and Elden, 195–197
hauntings
America's Stonehenge, 116–119
Brattleboro Retreat Tower, 184–185
Colonel Buck's memorial, 193–194
Conimicut Lighthouse, 140–142
Emily's Bridge, 158–159
Haunted Lake, 103–107
haunted stove, New Milford, 19–20
heads on Kickemuit River, 144–145
Knights's ghost in Maine, 194
Lizzie Borden Bed-and-Breakfast, 44–46
Mark Twain's mansion, 6–7
The Mount, Edith Wharton's home, 72–74
Mt. Tom, moaning bones, 148
Mt. Washington Hotel, 80–81
the Notchland Inn, 110–113
Opera House at Boothbay Harbor, 214–215
piano in Gardner Lake, 36–38
Pittsford Police Academy, 182–183
Portland Head Lighthouse, 190–191
Ram Tail Factory, 146
See also ghosts
Haviland, William, 188
Hawley, Massachusetts, 64
headless corpse, 135–137
heads on Kickemuit River, 144–145
headstones
of Captain Gray, 18
of Caroline Cutter, 76–77
of David Sherman, 4–5
of Elizabeth Mortimer Palmer, 132–133
of Ethan Allen, 180
in Flavor Graveyard, Vermont, 164–166
of Harvey Ball, 58
moved to make Williams Memorial Park, 21–23
of Nathan Selee, 61
of Peleg Walker, 146–147
of Spaudling's in Vermont, 175–177
See also cemeteries
Heartbreak House (Hearthside House), Rhode Island, 128–131
hermits
English Jack, 82–84
Ray Phillips, 216–218
See also vagabonds
Herrick, Rhoda D., 25–26
Hicks, Albert, 142–143
Hill, Betty and Barney, 120–122
Hinsdale, Massachusetts, 65
Hobbomock, 10–12
Holden, Maine, 197–199
Holden Hearse (Hoodoo Hearse), 197–199
Hooper, Brad, 195
Hopkins, Neil, 142
house, moving across frozen lake, 36–38
Hubbard, John E., 160–161
Hurricane Lake, Maine, 218–219
hurricane of 1938, 23, 149

I

Ice Age frog, 181
idiot failing upward, 68–71
immortal Doc Benton, 98–99
Ipswich, Massachusetts, 197
Iroquois people, 173

J

Jack, Weiner, 205
James Maury whaling ship, 18–19
Jobildunk Ravine, 98
Josselyn, John, 51
Judson, Theodore, 12, 14

K

Kelley, Joseph, 100–103
Kickemuit River, Rhode Island, 144–145
Kidd, Captain, 143
King, Frank, 27
King Philip's War, 144
Knight, in Westford, 40–42
Knights, Bill, 194
Knights of Pythias, 215

L

Lake Champlain, Vermont, 173–175, 178
Lake Memphremagog, Vermont, 185–187
landslide disaster, 95–97
lantern in window, 93–94
Lapp, Michael, 178
Lassen, Ken, 17
Lassen, Louis, 15, 17

laughing to death, 134
Leaping Logger syndrome, 209–210
Leavitt, Burton, 10
Lebanon, Connecticut, 18–19
Lecount, Thomas, 36, 38
legends, 1–2
Leicester, Vermont, 171
Lenox, Massachusetts, 72–74
Leominster, Massachusetts, 46–47
Lewis, Archie, 52
lighthouses
Conimicut, Rhode Island, 140–142
Portland Head, 190–191
on Stratford Point, Connecticut, 12–14
lightning strike, 4–5
Lilley, Arthur, 51
Lilley, Clara Bonney, 50–51
Lincoln, Enoch, 202–204
Lincoln, New Hampshire, 120–122
Lincoln, Rhode Island, 128–131
Little Compton, Rhode Island, 131–133
Little Maggie, 185–187
"Live Free or Die," 75
Lizzie Borden Bed-and-Breakfast, 44–46
Lobster Lake, specter moose, 210–211
lolly pops, 3
Longfellow, Henry Wadsworth, 62, 190
Louis's Lunch restaurant, 15–17
loup-garou (werewolf), 138–139
Lovecraft, H. P., 117, 118
Lover's Leap, Rhode Island, 152–153
Lowell, Massachusetts, 50–51, 206
lumberjacks
booze and Razor Shins, 211
leaping, in central Maine, 209–210
Paul Bunyan, 192
tale of the billdad, 218–219
Lyndeborough, New Hampshire, 107–109

M

Maine, ix, 189
Manana Island, Maine, 216–218
Marsh, Anna Hunt, 184
Marshall, Herbert, 29
Marshfield, Massachusetts, 52
Massachusetts, vii, 39
Mather, Cotton, 31, 32
Mazuroski, Steven, 174–175
McClure, David, 187–188
McKenna, Sheila, 204
Mead, George, 170
Mercer, Frederic W., 23
Meriden, Connecticut, 27–29
mermaid of Stratford Point Lighthouse, 14
Metacomet, Pokanoket Sachem, 144
Middlebury, Vermont, 170
Middletown, Rhode Island, 152–153
Milford, New Hampshire, 76–77
Mill Pond, Massachusetts, 59–60
mills
Foster Woolen Manufactory, Rhode Island, 146
at Haunted Lake, 105, 107
sawmill, Easton, Massachusetts, 59–60
textile, Smith Manufacturing Company, 128, 131
mines in Vermont, and Ice Age frog, 181
missile, Redstone, 78–80
moaning bones of Mt. Tom, 148
Molasses Flood, 47–49
Monhegan Island, Maine, 216–218
monsters. *See* beasts
Montpelier, Vermont, 160–161
monuments
Black Agnes, 160–161
Colonel Buck, 193–194
crank telephone, 195–197
Ethan Allen, 178–180
Governor Lincoln, 202–204
Joseph Palmer, 46–47
King Philip's War, 144–145
landslide disaster, 95–97
Phineas Gage medical miracle, 172–173
smiley face, 57–59
Westford Knight, 40–42
Willey boulders, 95–97
Witch Bonney, 50–51
See also statues
moose, specter, of Lobster Lake, 210–211
Moosehead Lake, Maine, 209–210
Morris, Connecticut, 17
Mortimer, Elizabeth, 132–133
Moultonborough, New Hampshire, 89
Mount, The, Massachusetts, 72–74
Moxie nerve tonic, 206–208
Mt. Carmel, Connecticut, 10–12
Mt. Katahdin, Maine, 212–213
Mt. Mansfield, Vermont, 167
Mt. Moosilauke, New Hampshire, 98–99
Mt. Tom, Rhode Island, 148
Mt. Washington Hotel, New Hampshire, 80–81
mummy, Egyptian, 170
murders
of Bill Knights, 194
at Great Falls National Bank, New Hampshire, 100–103
at Haunted Lake, 103, 105
Lizzie Borden's parents, 44–46
of peddler on Mt. Tom, 148
shoebox mystery, 23–25
Murphy, Bill, 219
Mystery Hill, America's Stonehenge, 117

N

Nancy Brook, 113
Narragansett Bay, Boston Neck, 154–156
Narrangansett rune stone, 149
Neil, T. J., 171
nerve tonics, 206–208
neurologists, and startle reflex, 209–210
New England Antiquities Research Association (NEARA), 149
New England Legends, x–xi, 225
New Hampshire, vii, 75
New Haven, Connecticut, 15–17, 30–32
New Haven, Vermont, 168–170
New London, Connecticut, 21–23
New Milford, Connecticut, 19–20
New Wrentham, Maine, 197–198
Newbury, New Hampshire, 84–86
Newburyport, Massachusetts, 68–71
Newburyport palace, 68–69, 71
Newport, Rhode Island, 134, 153
Newport, Vermont, 185–187
Nordic runes, 149
North America, Sinclair's expedition to, 40–42
North Kingstown, Rhode Island, 149, 153
Notchland Inn, New Hampshire, 110, 113
nutmeg spice, 3

O

observation tower, Rhode Island, 154–156
Old Harbor Road, Westport, Massachusetts, 42–44
Old Man of the Mountain, 75, 120
Old North Church, Boston, Massachusetts, 66–68
O'Neil-Gittens, Joan, 170
Opera House, Maine, 214–215
Oriental Tea Company, 53
Oxford Telephone Company, 195, 197

P

Paine, Thomas, 143
Palardy, Hawk, 19–20
Palmer, Joseph, 46–47

Palmer, Simeon, 131–133
Pamola, 213
Patten, Matthew, 105
Paul Bunyan, 192
Pemberton, John S., 208
Penobscot Expedition, 193
Penobscot Indians, 213
Perham, Dave, 195
petroglyphs in Vermont, 187–188
Phillips, Ray, 216–218
pianos, 36–38, 215
Pierpont, James, 31–32
pirates, 142–143
Piscataquis, Maine, 210–211
Pittsford, Vermont, 182–183
Pittsford Sanatorium for Tuberculosis, 182–183
plants, love of, 128, 131
plaques and signs
  Battle of the Frogs, 9–10
  Chicken Farmer sign, 84–86
  crank telephone, 197
  Old North Church rope flying, 67–68
  skeleton in armor, 62
  UFO encounter, 122
Pojac Point, Rhode Island, 149
Pokanoket people, 144
Police Academy, Vermont, 182–183
Ponaganset River, 146
Portsmouth, New Hampshire, 120–122
Potter, William, 146
Power, Marjory, 188
pranks
  bed warmers and coal shipment, 70–71
  booze and Razor Shins, 211
  fork in the road, 43
  haunted stove, 19–20
  Hoodoo Hearse, 199
  Ripton, Massachusetts, 64–65
  startle reflex in lumberjacks, 209–210
Pratt, D. D., 76–77
Prohibition, booze and Razor Shins, 211
Providence, Rhode Island, 124–125, 134
Purgatory Chasm, Rhode Island, 152–153
Purgatory Falls, New Hampshire, 107–109
Pynchon, William H. C., 27–29

Q

Queen Connie, giant gorilla, 170
Quinnipiac people, 10, 12

R

railroad construction accident, 172–173
Rak, Chuck, 205
Ram Tail Factory, Rhode Island, 146–147
Razor Shins, 211
Redstone missile, 78–80
Rhode Island, viii, 123
Rhode Island Horticultural Society, 131
Richmond, Ann Eddy, 124–125
Ripton, Massachusetts, 64–65
Robinson, Hannah, 154–156
rock carvings
  Dogtown's boulders, 54–57
  Nordic runes, 149
  petroglyphs in Vermont, 187–188
  Ship Stone, 42
  Westford Knight, 40
  See also boulders
rocking horses, 220
Rockport, Massachusetts, 51–52, 54
Rogers, Frank, 181
rope flying, 67–68
Rule, Gretchen, 84, 86
rum barrel as casket, 18–19
rune stone in Narrangansett, 149
Russell, Charles A., 51
Russell, Eliza and Amzi, 93
Russell, Ruth Priscilla, 93–94
Russell, Thomas, 93

S

Saco River, 95, 97, 113
Salem, Connecticut, 36–38
Salem, New Hampshire, 117–118
Salisbury, John, 144
Sandwich, New Hampshire, 87–89
satanic imps, 59–60
Schmitt, Tom, 42–44
Schoolcraft, Henry, 188
Scoby, David, 105, 107
sea serpents
  Champ, the Lake Monster, 173–175
  of Gloucester and Rockport, 51–52
  of Stratford Point Lighthouse, 12
  See also beasts
Selee, John, 59
Selee, Nathan, 59–61
Sestero, Nat A., 25
Sheldon, Henry, 170
Shepard, Alan, 78
Sherman, David, 4–5
Sherri, Antoinette, 114–115
Ship Stone, 42
ships, whaling, 18–19
shipwrecks, 190
shoebox murder mystery, 23–25
Simmonds, Bill, 82, 84
Simmonds, Mary, 82, 84
Simon, Benjamin, 122
Simon, Peter, 154–156
Sinclair, Prince Henry, 40–42
Sistine Chapel of Maine, 200–201
skeletons, 62–63, 105
Skinner, Maine, 218–219
Skowhegan School of Painting and Sculpture, 200–201
Sleeper, Cleveland Jr., 189
Sleeping Giant, 10–12
smiley face, 57–59
Smith, Ellsworth and Nellie, 140–142
Smith, George, 3
Smith, Stephen Hopkins, 128–131
Smith, Timothy Clark, 168–170
Somersworth, New Hampshire, 100–103
South Kingstown, Rhode Island, 154–156
South Solon, Maine, 200–201
South Solon Meeting House, 200–201
Southern Connector project, 162–164
Spaulding, Josiah, 175–177
Spaulding, Margaret, 175–177
specter moose of Lobster Lake, 210–211
Staples, Abigail, 126–127
Staples, Stephen, 126–127
Starbucks, 53
Stark, John (General), 75
Stark, John (historian), 62
State Mutual Insurance, 59
statues
  of Black Agnes, 160–161
  of Champ, the Lake Monster, 174–175
  of crank telephone, 195–197
  of frogs on bridge, 8–10
  on Great Wall of Sandwich, 87–89
  at Newburyport palace, 68–71
  of Paul Bunyan, 192
  of Queen Connie, giant gorilla, 170
  of Westford knight, 40–42
  of Witch Bonney, 50–51
  See also monuments
Steinhaus, Dan, 134
Stickney, Carolyn, 80–81
Stickney, Joseph (banker), 100
Stickney, Joseph (hotel builder), 80
Stoker, Bram, 126
Stonehenge, America's, 116–119
Stowe, Vermont, 158–159
Stratford, Connecticut, 12–14
Strout, Joseph, 190
Swasey, Parchie, 100
Swett, Ben H., 122
Swindell, Jim, 110, 113

T

taphephobia, 168–170
Tarr, Albert W., 52
Tatoskok (great serpent) , 173
tea kettle, 53
telephones, crank and rotary, 195–197
Terrill, Edward, 23, 24
Thomas, Lowell, 26
Thompson, Augustin, 206–208
Thoreau, Henry David, 213
thunderbird, 213
totem poles, 162
Tourette, Georges Gilles de la, 210
Tourette's syndrome, 210
towers
  Brattleboro Retreat Tower, 184–185
  brokenhearted, Rhode Island, 154–156
  "File Under...," 162–164
  US Air Force, in Ripton, 64
  See also lighthouses
treasure, buried at Page Farm, 143
Trudel, Harold A., 150
tuberculosis, 126, 156, 175–177, 182–183
Twain, Mark, 6–7

U

UFOs
  Allagash incident, 205
  Bantam Lake, craft crash, 17
  Betty and Barney Hill's incident, 120–122
  Boston, first documented, 71
  Buff Ledge Camp abduction, 178
  Woonsocket encounters, 150–151
Union, Maine, 206–208
US Air Force, 64, 122, 213
US Army, 78–80
US Civil War, medical innovations, 206

V

vagabonds
  Darn Man, 35–36
  Little Maggie, 185–187
  Thomas Colbath, 93–94
  See also hermits
vampires, 126–127, 177
Vermont, viii, 157
Vermont Asylum for the Insane, 184–185
Vials, John Alfred "Jack," 82–84
Volkswagen Beetle, 170

W

Walker, Mrs. Joshua, 134
Walker, Peleg, 146–147
Wall, Great, of Sandwich, 87–89
Wallingford, Connecticut, 23–25
Wampahoofus, 167
Wampanoag Indians, 62
Warren, New Hampshire, 78–80
Warren, Rhode Island, 144–145
Warwick, Rhode Island, 140–142
wasting disease. *See* tuberculosis
water fountain, 124–125
Waterbury, Vermont, 164–166
Webb, Walter, 178
Weiner, Jack and Jim, 205
werewolf of Woonsocket, 138–139
West Athens, Maine, 194
Westford, Massachusetts, 40–42
Westford Knight, 40–42
Westport, Massachusetts, 42–44
whaling ships, 18–19
Wharton, Edith, 73–74
Wharton, Edward Robbins, 73
Wheeler, William, 4
Whipple, Joseph, 110, 113
White Mountains
  and English Jack, 82–84
  landslide disaster, 95–97
  and Mt. Moosilauke, 98–99
  and Mt. Washington Hotel, 80–81
  and the Notchland Inn, 110–113
  UFO incident in, 120
Whitman, Gil, 196–197
Willey, Benjamin, 97
Willey, Samuel Jr. and Polly, 95–97
Willeys, the, 95–97
Williams, Charles Augustus, 21
Williams, Edward H., 172–173
Williams, Joshua, 152
Williams, Ted, 208
Willimantic, Connecticut, 8–10
Windham, Connecticut, 8–10
Windham County, Connecticut, 35–36
Winthrop, John, 71
Wislocki, George, 65
Witch Bonney, 50–51
witch's curse on Buck's grave, 193–194
Wood, Mary, 135
Woodstock, Maine, 195–197
Woonsocket, Rhode Island, 138–139, 150–151
Worcester, Massachusetts, 57–59
Worley, Harry, 20

Y

York, Sumner D., 52

About Jeff Belanger

Jeff Belanger is an award-winning author, podcaster, storyteller, adventurer, and explorer of the unexplained. He's written more than a dozen books, including *The World's Most Haunted Places, The Fright Before Christmas,* and his memoir *The Call of Kilimanjaro.* He's the award-winning, Emmy-nominated host, writer, and producer of the *New England Legends* series on PBS and Amazon Prime. He also hosts the *New England Legends* weekly podcast, which has garnered over six million downloads since it was launched in 2017. He provides live programs and performances to audiences all over the world, and he's been the writer and researcher for every episode of Ghost Adventures on the Discovery Channel since the show premiered in 2008. He's the founder and publisher of *Shadow Zine,* and he's been a guest on hundreds of radio and television networks and programs, making regular appearances on the Discovery Channel's Shock Docs, the History Channel's *The UnXplained with William Shatner,* plus he's been featured on networks and programs like the Travel Channel, PBS, NECN, Living TV (UK), the *CBS News Early Show, CBS Sunday Morning,* Sunrise 7 (Australia), FOX, NBC, ABC, and CBS affiliates, National Public Radio, the BBC, Australian Radio Network, and *Coast to Coast AM.*

Websites: *JeffBelanger.com* | *OurNewEnglandLegends.com* | *ShadowZine.com* | *Ghostvillage.com*
Facebook: @ExploringLegends
Instagram: @ExploringLegends
YouTube: @LegendTripping

About Frank Grace

Frank Grace turns renowned, infamous, and peculiar landmarks into stylized, yet creepy, works of art. He has been photographing weird and wonderful New England since 2010. He combines his camera and eye with Photoshop manipulation to bring out the surreal aspects of his subjects.

He's been a finalist for Ron Howard's *Project Imagination* in 2010 and 2011, and his work has been shown in galleries in both New England and New York. Some of Frank's images will be headed to the moon on the Astrobotic Griffin Lander/NASA VIPER Rover to be part of the Lunar Codex in the "Polaris Collection—Lunar South Pole." His contributions to the Lunar museum are included in the summer 2022 edition of *O Muse!: Art, Literature & Music* magazine. His photography has appeared in many books, several magazines, including *Playboy,* and other publications, and is featured in the stage show and PBS documentary *An Evening of Ghost Stories and New England Legends.* He loves all things ghostly and strange. Since 2014, he's published the annual *Haunted New England* wall calendar with Jeff Belanger.

Website: *TrigPhotography.com*
Facebook: @TrigPhotography
Instagram: @Frank_C_Grace